Inventory

Strategy

RightStock™

Maximizing Financial, Service, and Operational Performance with Inventory Strategy

Inventory Strategy

Edward H. Frazelle, Ph.D.

LOGISTICS RESOURCES
INTERNATIONAL INC

RightChain™

Copyright

ISBN 978-0-9857463-0-8

Logistics Resources International
1266 West Paces Ferry Road
Atlanta, GA 30327 USA
Phone: 678-653-9807
Email: EdFrazelle@LRIConsulting.com
Web1: LRIConsulting.com
Web2: RightChain.com
Blog: InventoryStrategy.com

Dedication

This book is dedicated to my Lord, Savior, Best Friend, and Teacher Jesus Christ Who blessed me with the experiences and abilities to share these lessons. This book is also dedicated to my gorgeous wife Pat, who for 27 years has patiently allowed me to have these experiences and encouraged me in them. Finally, this book is dedicated to our two children, Kelly and Andrew; none finer.

Acknowledgements

I have been blessed for many years with wise, patient, and supportive business partners. I know them now better as friends. I am eternally grateful to Hugh Kinney, Juan Rubio, Masaji Nakano, Ricardo Sojo, Tammy Artosky, Harvey Donaldson, Lou Arace, and Steve Westphal who have been in many supply chain trenches with me and invested much of themselves in me.

I am also fortunate to have two long term joint venture partnerships that have worked with me to advance our field and serve a global client base. Our joint venture with Mitsubishi dates back many years. I am very grateful to Fujimoto-san, Kawakami-san, Matsukawa-san, Shibuya-san, and Takeushi-san for their excellent and diligent work, hospitality, friendship and business integrity.

We also work in close partnership with GS1 Peru. That team of highly effective professionals has become my Peruvian family. I will always be thankful to Angel Becerra, Mary Wong, Patricio Blanco, and Violeta Vargas for the many doors they have opened for me.

As you will be able to tell from the book, I definitely have a nerd side. That side has been developed through long-standing relationships with two of the world's top academic institutions – Georgia Tech and Waseda University. I do not have words to express my appreciation for the opportunities they have afforded me.

We all need mentors and coaches. My professional mentors and coaches are the best I have ever known. Dr. John White, Mr. Jun Suzuki, Dr. John Jarvis, and Dr. Teruo Takahashi took me under their wings and served as inspiring role models.

In LRI's supply chain strategy consulting and training, we are exceedingly blessed to work alongside some of the world's most outstanding individuals. They have encouraged me professionally and personally, and have helped us develop and share our RightChain™ principles, processes, and tools. I am very grateful for the privilege they have provided us to consider their supply chain and inventory issues. There are too many folks to name here but I do want to highlight a "few" special ones.

- Luis Alvarez and 3M.
- Carlos Carbajal, Armando Coral and Alicorp.
- Steve Laky, Emil Jivan, Rick Glassey and Abbott.
- Steve Spiva and Applied Materials.
- Jane Howse, Bill Hightower and AT&T/BellSouth.
- Roosevelt Tolliver and Avon.
- Peter Post and BIC.
- Jack Davis, Aaron Tappan and Bloomberg.
- Carliss Graham, Greg Otter, Durwood Knight, Richard McCrosky, Raylene Carter, Frank Slaughter, Caroline Thompson and BP.
- Michael Cardone and Cardone Industries.
- Pete Dragich, Diane Mullican and Carrier.
- Dave Hopkins, Steve Westphal, Brett Frankenberg, Kevin Fox, Ted Bozarth, and Coca-Cola Consolidated.
- Hal Welsh, Lynn Barratt, Steve Erbe, Carmen Guerrero, Karen Hall, Tom Nabbe, Bruce Terry, Peggy Shiver, John Byron and Disney.
- Jim Dailey, Stan John, Dwight Grant, Sixto Porras and Focus on the Family
- Robert Pickerill, Jill Schaade and GE.
- Dan Krouse and Hallmark.

- Sean Garrett, Dave Eidam and Hamilton Sundstrand.
- Jim Roach, Bruce Smith, Juan Streeter, Kathy Howell, Tony Gomes, Chuck Hamilton, Tammy Elliott and Honda.
- Jim Teal and H.P. Hood.
- Dave Wilford and Invitrogen/Life Sciences.
- Debbie Postle and LAM Research.
- Mike Harry, Randy Brough and Lifeway.
- Susan McClain and LL Bean.
- Sid Henderson, Bart Mangum, Brad Morris and Nuskin.
- Lou Arace, Joe Boileau, Dave Burton and Nutrisystem.
- Darrell Pavelqua, Mary Boatright, Dave Milton, James Wichern and Payless.
- Steve Baker and PetSafe.
- Danny DiPerna, Cathy Godin, Ismail Mokabel, Lisa Michaud, Dennis Reinholt and Pratt & Whitney.
- Mario Lalonde and P&G.
- Frank Encinas, Kristan Even, Mark Ward and Raytheon.
- Scott Singer, Russell Hodson and Rio Tinto.
- Sean Stucker, Bill Burgess, Greg Flack, Greg Olsem, Vicki Schwarz and Schwan's.
- Toni Darby, Reuben Welch and SKC.
- Eric Eber, Mike Graska, Matt LoPicolo, Amelia Pickerill, Nick Lubar and Swagelok.
- Sam Campagna, Jackie Dematos, Jan Salewski and United Technologies.
- Matt Anderson, Tony Fuller and the U.S. Army.
- Carlos and Rodrigo Uribe and Wal-Mart Central America.

THANKS!

Preface

I have been consulting, teaching, and researching in supply chain strategy for 30+ years. I have traveled in more than 72 countries, worked in countless industries, and faced what seems to be the full gauntlet of supply chain issues. Over the past three years The Lord led me through a series of very intense projects with a common focus - inventory. From mining, to food, to aerospace, to retail, to electronics, to computing, to CPG, to bottling – in North America, South America, Europe, and Asia... nearly every project had inventory optimization at the heart of it. In addition, many of the projects resulted in *highly profitable increases in inventory* levels. In one amazing sequence of projects the very DC we helped Hallmark close as a part of their inventory reduction was acquired by Coca-Cola Consolidated as a part of our inventory expansion with them.

I am not normally led through those type of themed experiences unless The Lord has a strong lesson for me and my clients in it. I asked Him what His message was for this time. He seemed to be saying "Inventory Strategy". I asked Him, Lord, why Inventory Strategy. He seemed to be saying, "because people are so consumed with reducing inventory in the face of circumstances where more is required that they are becoming overwhelmed. My Ways are not those of lack and lean, but of abundance and blessing. What some call waste, I call margin; the margin needed to balance life at work, life with family, and life with Me. What some call "waste", I call an opportunity to generously give to others."

He also does not seem to be too happy with inventory shell games that go on and the idolatry of companies known for their inventory prowess who have hidden their inventory in their supplier's warehouses.

In the middle of this year I hit an unusual lull between projects. To fill the time I began to write a playbook on inventory management requested by one of our clients. At The Lord's prompting, the playbook slowly started to take the form of a real book. That's what you are reading. An inventory playbook demonstrating that less is not always more; more is not always less; and **run the numbers to figure it out**.

I have watched highly effective professionals struggle with the decision of how much inventory to carry. They are beat up, thrown under the bus, and sometimes let go if they have too much inventory, too little inventory, or can't figure out where to locate it. The struggle often comes because inventory is a business matter, a financial matter, a service matter, and an operational matter. Inventory levels also are related to the performance of manufacturing, procurement, transportation, and sales. Sometimes inventory is an asset and sometimes a liability. All are true. The inability to rationalize and optimize inventory across those interdependent and fluctuating concerns is normally the root of the conflicts and strife. *Inventory Strategy* and our RightStock™ model are attempts to unify and rationalize those often conflicting views and perspectives.

After I taught this approach in a recent seminar in Tokyo I had an unusual question from a lady in the audience. She asked, "Dr. Frazelle, if we figure this out, what will we do with our time?" I could tell The Lord wanted to speak directly to her and many in the audience. He gave me a vision of the late and sleepless nights she was enduring under the stress and how much her family needed her and missed her. I responded, "Ma'am, inventory is not a hill worth dying on. When you apply this approach, you can spend time with your family and God and take some time to rest." She and my translator started to cry. Even I started to tear up. There is a way through these issues that does not require the 7x24x365 strain that so many supply chain professionals work under. This book is my best attempt to show a less stressful and more peaceful way through the myriad and maze-like issues inherent to inventory and supply chain strategy.

Over the last 20+ years the RightStock™ approach to inventory strategy has been applied in nearly every industry in nearly every part of the world. I have taught it to thousands of professionals in many different languages. So far it is responsible for more than $1 Billion in profit improvements and a lot more personal and professional peace. The approach uses data, analytics, and a proven methodology to maximize the financial, service, and operational performance of inventory. In sharing it here I will use the best mix of examples, analogies, and analytics that I can put together to present the RightStock™ principles, methodology, and tools.

Lastly, thank you for taking the time and energy to read *Inventory Strategy*. I would appreciate any and all constructive feedback. Since the book is published electronically and in print on-demand I can edit the book on the fly to enhance it for future readers.

I can be reached via email at EdFrazelle@LRIConsulting.com.

In addition, comments may be posted at InventoryStrategy.com. The blog site also provides education versions of some of the simulations illustrated in the book.

Contents

List of Figures

Chapter 1

Chapter 2

Inventory Strategy

Chapter 1

Introduction

RightChain™

A few years ago I conducted a workshop for the operating committee of one of the world's largest industrial conglomerates. The heads of operations for each business unit plus the company's COO participated. We had a question and answer session at the end of the workshop. The COO asked the first question. "Dr. Frazelle, we have quite a bit of conflict in these meetings. Especially lately. Why is that?" I asked him what the charter of the group was. He said, "We have two main objectives. The first is to reduce inventory. The second is to lower our unit costs." I said politely, "You just answered your own question. Your main methods of reducing unit cost, global sourcing from cheap labor sources and buying in large quantities to receive discounts, increase your inventory levels. Your objectives are at odds with one another so you are at odds with one another." He asked me what they should do about it. I encouraged them, like I encourage all our clients, to take a step back and reconsider their objectives and their approach. I suggested that their objectives would preferably be to maximize return on invested capital (ROIC), improve perfect order percentage, spend whatever was required in total supply chain cost to support those objectives, and invest in whatever inventory level was required to accomplish those objectives. Sometimes that inventory level will be higher and sometimes it will be lower. *Inventory is not an end in itself; it is a means to an end.*

We encounter this conflict in nearly every client situation. In all but the wisest and most mature organizations, highly qualified professionals are required to do the impossible; respond to a barrage of typically uncoordinated and irreconcilable initiatives from across the organization. Those initiatives normally include many of the following. Increase SKUs. Increase customization. Increase inventory availability. Reduce customer response times. Reduce transportation costs. Reduce purchase costs through global sourcing. Reduce manufacturing costs. Mitigate increasing supply chain risk with multiple sources. All of these naturally work to increase inventory levels. Yet, facing prevailing lean thinking, most supply chain professionals are still required to reduce inventory.

A few months ago the head of logistics from one of the world's leading computing industry companies called in tears over the impossible situation they had been placed in. That was a first: inventory angst to the point of tears.

1.1 What's the Problem?

The inventory conundrum is exacerbated by many complicating factors. We categorize the factors into five major malfunctions:

- Data Discrepancies
- Inadequate Training & Education
- Problematic Perspectives
- Misaligned Metrics
- Poisonous Paradigms

Data Discrepancies

1. **Base Data Errors**. In many companies the base data used to control and plan inventory and to support inventory decision making is *just plain wrong*. In a recent project with one of the world's most prominent HVAC firms we discovered that more than 50% of the MRP, bill of materials (BOM), and on-hand inventory records were wrong. In a recent engagement with a large engine manufacturer we found that inventory planners were regularly manipulating historical demand, set points and parameters to falsify turn rates .

2. **Un-vetted Changes**. It is not unusual to find hundreds of people, qualified and unqualified, with and without accountability, making un-vetted changes to schedules, demand, supplier data, and MRP data. We recently came across a client situation where more than 500 people had access to make changes to multi-million dollar assembly schedules. With a large retailer we found that more than 300 people had clearance to modify multi-million dollar store order replenishment schemes.

Inadequate Training & Education

3. **Untrained Planners**. Based on my experience I estimate that less than 30% of inventory planners and analysts working with inventory systems have any formal education in inventory management. During a recent project I asked to see the resumes of the inventory planners. Less than 10%

had any formal training in the decisions they were making. Many people pulling inventory triggers don't know how to use the gun.

4. **Faulty Fundamentals**. Because so few inventory planners and managers have inventory training and education, *there is widespread misunderstanding and misapplication of inventory management fundamentals*. During a recent engagement with a large healthcare company I asked about their inventory accuracy. They said that it was well above 98%. I was suspicious, so I asked them how they defined inventory accuracy. They said it was the portion of demand shipped from inventory. I explained that that was fill rate, not inventory accuracy. I then asked what their inventory accuracy was. They didn't know.

Problematic Perspectives

5. **Conflicting Perspectives**. Every inventory decision impacts financial, service, and operational performance. However, very few individuals understand all three and very few decision support tools consider all three. As a result, different inventory levels appear high or low depending on the glasses you're wearing. Those views need to be reconciled; a major point and objective of this book.

6. **Irreconcilable Interdependencies**. Decisions made in customer service, inventory management, manufacturing, sourcing, transportation, and warehousing all work

RightChain™

interdependently to impact inventory levels. However, very few individuals understand those interdependencies and very few decision support tools consider them.

7. **Operations Myopia**. Inventory is typically viewed as an operational or tactical outcome. Inventory is rarely viewed as a strategic contributor to an overall supply chain strategy which in turn serves as a part of an integrated business strategy.

8. **Misplaced   Accountability**. *Many   people   influence inventory levels but often no one is accountable*. I like to ask our clients early on who is accountable for inventory. The answer is revealing and quickly highlights the organizational and measurement root of inventory and/or supply chain issues.

9. **No Microscopes**. Every SKU has a unique demand pattern, supply pattern, and dimensional profile. Individual SKUs are bought, sold, and slotted. Yet, most companies resist individual SKU inventory optimization and planning. Even in cases with 100,000+ SKUs we have developed individual SKU strategies and rolled those up into category and business unit inventory strategies. Inventory strategy is a top-down AND bottom-up endeavor. Wide angle lens AND microscopes are required and available.

Misaligned Metrics

10. **Traditional Accounting**. Traditional accounting treats inventory strictly as an asset whereas operationally and philosophically inventory is popularly considered a liability.

11. **Conflicting Metrics**. Metrics used in the five supply chain logistics activities – customer service, inventory management, sourcing, transportation, and warehousing – often work at odds with one another and yield excess inventory.

Poisonous Paradigms

12. **Procurement "Cost Avoidance"**. In the name of "cost avoidance", procurement is still looking for the cheapest first price that may cost much more in related excess inventory carrying costs.

13. **Lean**. Lean literature and previously idolized supply chain operators often veil the fact that their inventory turn advantages typically come at the expense of suppliers further up the chain.

Were it not for poor fundamentals, grasping for silver bullets, limited education, misaligned metrics, myopic perspectives, misplaced influence and accountability, misalignment with corporate strategy, and false prevailing paradigms: developing inventory strategy would be a piece of cake.

RightChain™

During a recent client workshop the chief supply chain officer noticed that I was becoming discouraged as they bemoaned their inventory ills. He said, "Dr. Frazelle, don't get discouraged. We don't. We just keep our heads down, keep making stuff, and hope it turns out OK in the end." Fortunately he was joking. Unfortunately many live in a world with their heads down, making and buying stuff, and hoping it turns out OK in the end. There has to be a better way.

1.2 More or Less

There are myriad interdependencies and complexities in inventory decision making. The complexity overwhelms and discourages many. They often give up and assume based on the prevailing winds of trade literature and stock analyst exhortations that less is better. Sometimes they are right. Sometimes they are wrong.

Lean thinking is so ingrained and influential that adding inventory is considered almost criminal, as if there is an inventory police force lurking around every decision to catch someone adding inventory to a supply chain. Yet, in several of the supply chain strategies we have recently completed the answer was to increase inventory levels: in each case leading to improved financial, service, and operational performance.

In a recent project with one of the world's most successful consumer products companies, well known for their inventory management, we found that financial metrics for inventory performance were not in place. When we used our RightStock™ financial metrics in combination with our service and operational metrics we found that the company was under-invested in inventory. Increasing the inventory investments helped the company gain significant market share, increase customer satisfaction, raise profits, and increase share price.

In a recent project with a large bottler we found that due to lean leanings and a proliferating SKU base, the company was running lot sizes half the size of optimal. Increasing lot sizes and related warehousing space led to significant reductions in total supply chain costs.

We are currently working with a large aerospace company on their supply chain strategy. The strategy revolves around one of the world's most advanced engine assembly facilities. After touring the facility I was asked what I thought about it. I shared my concern that the facility had been built under an assumption of a nearly guaranteed, steady cadence of supply and demand; which given the global and competitive dynamics was unreasonable. It appears that a greater inventory investment will be required to operate their supply chain.

A few years ago we worked with a large provider of financial services software and terminals. The annual revenue related to each terminal dwarfs the annual inventory investment required to keep each terminal operating. Despite previous attempts to lean out the inventory, we found the inventory strategy required a much larger number of relatively inexpensive mice, keyboards, terminals, and cables to guarantee that terminal downtime impacting multi-million and sometimes multi-billion dollar decisions was not an issue.

I could keep going, but I believe you get the picture. ***Sometimes the answer is more inventory***. Sometimes the answer is less.

Honda

We have been fortunate to work with Honda for many years. Our work with them began when Jim Roach, their head of sales and service, attended one of our supply chain strategy seminars. I was curious as to why such a high level executive was in our seminar. He explained that he had complained so much about the performance of their supply chain that their president finally assigned it to him. To his credit he invested himself and his team in learning and implementing the RightChain™ and RightStock™ models.

Through a year of intense work in SKU rationalization, customer service optimization, forecasting improvements, dramatic leadtime reductions including daily delivery programs to dealerships nationwide and weekly delivery programs from suppliers worldwide, and significant process and WMS improvements in their nine DCs – a success story was born. The story is illustrated in Figure 1.1. Historically when there was a downturn in service, inventory levels were simply raised to close the gap with target fill rates. When inventory levels were deemed too high, they were systematically reduced creating unacceptably low fill rates. That cycle went on, as it does in many companies, for many years. Once the RightStock™ model kicked in, inventory levels were cut in half; from 6 months on-hand to 3 months on-hand. Fill rates increased dramatically as well; growing from a low of 96% to a high of 99%. The business results included reducing inventory investments by tens of millions of dollars, increasing profitability to the point where their business unit became the most profitable in Honda, and improving service to the point where Honda led all industry related service categories.

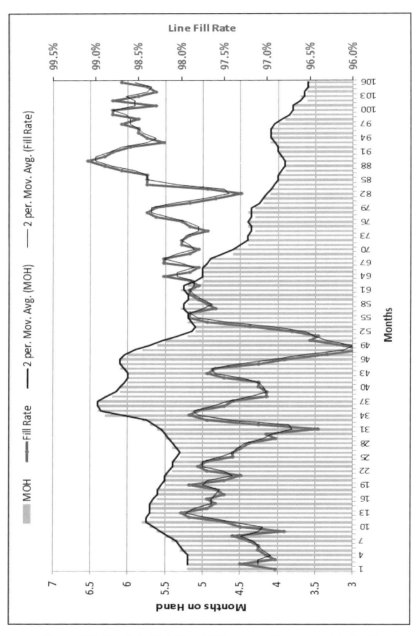

Figure 1.1 Honda's RightStock™ Journey. From worst to first!

Hallmark

Our work with Hallmark began with a call asking for assistance locating a new distribution center. We asked why they needed the new distribution center. They said that inventory levels had grown to the point where they had exceeded their network's storage capacity. We asked them why their inventory was growing so quickly. They shared that they had been increasing their SKUs in hopes of increasing sales but that sales had remained flat. When we revealed to them the reduction in return on invested capital and shareholder value related to the potential DC, they took a step back. To make a long RightSKUs™ story short, after optimizing the SKU base and related inventories, we determined they needed only about 60% of their existing inventory and related storage space. That led to the closing of two major DCs. In a strange twist of inventory fate, one of those DCs was acquired by our bottling client who needed to increase their inventory levels in that locale (Figure 1.2).

Figure 1.2 Sometimes more and sometimes less.
The principle manifested in this 233,000 square foot DC in Raleigh, NC
vacated by Hallmark and acquired by Coca-Cola Consolidated.

Depending on many factors and interdependencies... Sometimes less inventory is needed; sometimes more. Sometimes the answer is the same inventory, invested differently. Sometimes the answer is different inventory. Sometimes the answer is the same inventory re-located. The only way I have ever been able to figure it out is to RUN THE NUMBERS!

Last year we worked with a large food company on their supply chain and inventory strategy. One of the project team meetings was unusually quiet. The COO pulled me aside after the meeting to talk about the team's participation. He shared that one of the team members shared with him that the group had become reticent to speak up because they assumed I always knew the answer to whatever inventory question was on the table. I shared with him and with the group that I rarely know the answer before we start a project. There are too many inter-related factors to know philosophically or in advance of putting the numbers to the scenario. What I do know is how to figure out what to do. We call that optimization.

1.3 Optimization

Optimization is a facet of our RightStock™ program that differentiates it from operational, quality, and/or philosophical approaches to inventory management. Those approaches include Lean, Six-Sigma, Pull, and Just-in-Time. Those approaches all have their roots in the Toyota Production System – and implicitly assume that inventory is waste, that perfect quality is always the goal, and that moving things between places more often is always better than carrying inventory.

Through optimization, we take into consideration the unique economic and competitive climate, financial goals, customer service requirements, logistics conditions, and culture of each business to help determine the right supply chain and inventory strategy. Though it may sound heretical, ***optimal strategies may require carrying more inventory***. That was the case in four of our largest and most successful supply chain strategy engagements last year. In each case, the strategic increase in inventory led to higher profits, higher market share, and higher levels of customer satisfaction. Though it may sound

RightChain™

heretical, the optimal solution may not mean perfect quality, but optimal quality. We use a computation of the cost (expense, capital, and lost revenue) of poor quality to help our clients determine the optimal level of quality and appropriate investments in quality improvements. Though it may sound heretical, optimal supply chain strategies may involve fewer, less frequent movements using less expensive transportation modes. It is the cost of fuel and freight relative to the cost of carrying inventory and the customer service requirement that should determine the frequency, length, and modes for supply chain moves – not the philosophical or operational paradigms of supply chain mantras.

Our RightStock™ model employs optimization as its basis for decision support. Optimization is a formal, data driven, decision support approach. It decomposes a decision into an objective function and constraints and conquers with a logical algorithm or heuristic. I have found it to be one of the most effective and reliable means of problem solving and decision support. I have also found that the concept escapes many professionals in our seminars and in our consulting projects. Let me take a stab at simplifying the concept.

How to get to California?

If I asked you to tell me the best way to travel from Atlanta to Los Angeles what would you say? When I ask that question in our seminars, most say by plane. When they respond so quickly they are making assumptions about the trip. They are assuming that there is sufficient money available to buy a plane ticket, that time is of the essence, and that air travel is preferred. (That says a lot about our culture.) The real answer is, "It depends."

Suppose I add something to the question and ask you to tell me the best way to go if you only have $100.00. What would you say? Now the range of options may be limited to hitch hiking or stowaway. Suppose I add that money is no object and that you have to be there within 12 hours. What would you say? Now the only option is to go by plane, and since money is no object, why not charter a jet? Suppose I say you have to be there in 12 hours and spend the least amount of money possible. What would you say? Now the range is even narrower and probably means getting the cheapest possible coach plane ticket. In that example, "12 hours" is a constraint and the "least amount of money possible" is the objective function. In optimization terms it would look like this:

- Objective Function = Minimize Total Money Spent
- Constraint(s) = Arrive within 12 Hours

⦿RightChain™

Without an objective function AND constraint(s), any answer is right and any answer is wrong. Since most business, supply chain, and inventory decisions are not framed with optimization; how are business, supply chain, or inventory decisions made? Unfortunately, it often comes down to who can write the most caustic email, who has the boss's ear, who has the most political clout, etc.

Inventory Objective Functions

An optimization statement is comprised of two components - an objective function and constraints. Isolated to inventory, the optimization becomes finding the inventory level that yields the best possible financial performance for the business and supply chain subject to fill rate, response time, shipping frequency, and storage capacity constraints.

The RightStock™ model uses a menu of objective functions for inventory decision optimization. They are all related to financial performance, and include the impact of inventory and fill rate on revenue, expense and capital. (This is a major departure from most supply chain philosophies, tools, and metrics which typically only consider the impact of decisions on expenses or operational performance indicators.) RightStock™ objective functions include maximizing Return on Invested Capital (ROIC), maximizing Inventory Value Added™ (IVA), minimizing Inventory Policy Cost (IPC), and maximizing Gross

Margin Return on Inventory (GMROI). There will be a much more comprehensive explanation of these objective functions in section 2.6.

Inventory Constraints

If all we had was an objective function, logistics optimization would be easy. Admittedly facetious, but regrettably common, here's a storyline that is played out in many companies. Let's consider each of the total logistics cost components (Figure 1.3), independently. First, transportation. Transportation has become so expensive and complex that we may just decide to stop trying. Fuel costs. Regulatory hassles. Poorly performing carriers. The list goes on. Second, warehousing. All the JIT, Lean, and Six Sigma books suggest that warehousing is non-value added, and just plain bad for business. Let's close the warehouses. Third, inventory carrying. Even though inventory is still an asset in accounting, we all know it's a liability (borderline illegal in some companies) and politically incorrect in the current JIT, Lean, Six Sigma environment. We need to stop carrying inventory. Since there is no inventory, there will be no customers, so lost sales cost is eliminated. These all work together to completely eliminate total logistics cost and the inventory that goes with it. We win, right? Wrong!

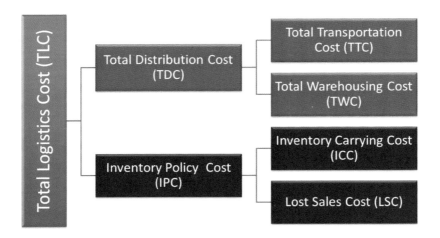

Figure 1.3 Total Logistics Cost Elements for Optimization

In addition to common sense, what should prohibit an
organization from going down that road to ruin? A customer
service policy (CSP). A RightChain™ Customer Service Policy is
segmented by channel, ABC customer class within a channel,
commodity, and SKU class within a commodity (Figure 1.4). The
customer service policy establishes targets which must be met
for fill rate, response time, delivery frequency, delivery quality,
packaging, and any other stipulated dimension of customer
service. Those requirements serve as constraints in supply chain
logistics optimization. An example supply chain logistics
optimization statement from a recent service parts client follows.

RightServe™ Customer Service Optimization System™

Channel	Customer Class	SKU Class	Shipment Preparation Time (Internal Prep Time)	Delivery Frequency (Time Between Deliveries)	Order Cutoff Time (Latest Time for Order Placement)	Fill Rate (Inventory Availability and Allocation Rules)
Channel I	A	A	Same Day Pickup- 9:00 AM	Twice Daily	10:00 PM	99.5% - Allocation
		B	Next Day - 12:00 PM	Daily	9:00 PM	98% - Allocation
		C	72 Hours	Weekly	8:00 PM	96% - Allocation
	B	A	Next Day - 12:00 PM	Daily	9:00 PM	99% - Right of Refusal
		B	Two-Day - 12:00 PM	Weekly	7:00 PM	94% - Right of Refusal
		C	Leadtime by SKU	Monthly	5:00 PM	91% - Right of Refusal
	C	A	Two-Day - 12:00 PM	Weekly	5:00 PM	Delayed Acknowledgement
		B	72 Hours	Monthly	3:00 PM	Delayed Acknowledgement
		C	One Week	Monthly	3:00 PM	Delayed Acknowledgement
Channel II	A	A	Next Day - 12:00 PM	Daily	7:00 PM	97.5% - Allocation
		B	Next Day - 12:00 PM	Daily	7:00 PM	93% - Allocation
		C	Two-Day - 12:00 PM	Weekly	6:00 PM	84% - Allocation
	B	A	72 Hours	Weekly	5:00 PM	94% - Right of Refusal
		B	72 Hours	Monthly	6:00 PM	89% - Right of Refusal
		C	One Week	Monthly	7:00 PM	77% - Right of Refusal
	C	A	One Week	Monthly	4:00 PM	Delayed Acknowledgement
		B	Leadtime by SKU	Monthly	5:00 PM	Delayed Acknowledgement
		C	Leadtime by SKU	Monthly	6:00 PM	Delayed Acknowledgement

Figure 1.4 Multi-Channel Customer Service Policy

RightChain™

Objective Function
- Minimize Total Logistics Cost

Constraints
1. Fill Rate ≥ 90%
2. Response Time ≤ 96 Hours
3. Delivery Frequency = 3x per Week
4. Shipping Accuracy ≥ 99.7%

An illustration of the optimization is in Figure 1.5. Note that the customer service policy yielding the lowest total logistics cost is a response time of 3 days and a fill rate of 99%. (That is not always the case and just happened to be for one particular SKU for this particular client.) The tricky part is that as fill rate increases, inventory carrying cost, warehousing costs, and potentially transportation costs increase while lost sales costs decrease. Those dynamics and interdependencies are reflected on one axis. As response time decreases, transportation costs, warehousing costs, and potentially inventory carrying costs increase (depending on whether the response time requirement is met via more expensive transportation or more warehousing close to the customer); but lost sales cost decrease. Those dynamics and interdependencies are reflected on the other axis.

A strictly inventory optimization statement would include one or more of the following objective functions and one or more of the following constraints. (Each will be explained in much more detail as we proceed through the book.)

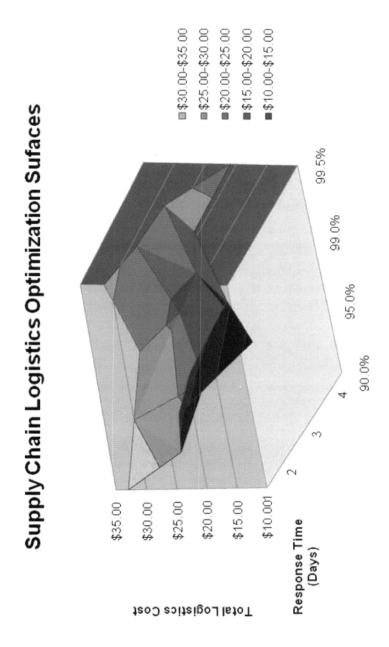

Figure 1.5 Supply Chain Logistics Optimization Surfaces

🐚 **RightChain™**

Inventory Objective Function Candidates

- Maximize Gross Margin Return on Inventory (GMROI)
- Maximize Inventory Value Added™ (IVA)
- Minimize Inventory Policy Cost™ (IPC)

Inventory Optimization Constraints

- Fill Rate ≥ Target
- Response Time ≤ Target
- Shipping Frequency ≥ Target
- Inventory ≤ Storage Capacity

Determining and implementing the inventory level that satisfies the required constraints and yields the best financial performance is inventory optimization.

1.4 To(o) Lean or not to(o) Lean?

As a part of the National Science Foundation's Japan Technology Evaluation Center I had the unique privilege to lead a major study for the U.S. government comparing U.S. and Japanese logistics systems. During the study I interviewed business and supply chain executives in many large Japanese organizations. Not surprisingly, one of those was Toyota. I spent significant time with the developers of the Toyota Production System and their professor. One of the stories they shared explains more about the Toyota Production System than all the books I have ever read on the topic.

The Toyoda (the company name was created from the family name) family was a rice farming family. They became wealthy when they invented mechanical harvesting equipment for rice. At some point they decided that if they could make rice harvesting equipment, they could also make cars. The production concepts did not translate very well and the auto making venture almost bankrupted the family. The head of the family decided to hire a new engineer from outside the family and gave him one year to develop a new way to make cars. To make a long story short, that young man came up with a way to profitably make cars in an island nation (self-contained), with few natural resources (no waste), limited habitable land (no space), and locust-like industrial congestion (perfectly orderly). The Toyota Production System was born out of those unique geographic, business, and cultural conditions.

Those are not the same conditions that exist in the United States, western Europe, eastern Europe, China, Mexico, Brazil, etc. (The head of supply chain for one of the major automotive companies operating in those other countries shared with me that they call lean, "anorexia".) There are many beneficial ideas and concepts in the Toyota Production System and its paradigm children, but they are not all applicable and they are not all best practices. They were for Toyota, but not for everyone. That's why we coined the phrase, "***Don't philosophize, optimize***!"

1.5 The Inventory Journey

Inventory Strategy is a journey through increasingly advanced inventory strategies and increasing levels of inventory management maturity. The book employs a comprehensive mix of case studies, analytics, and illustrations to confront prevailing inventory paradigms, re-establish the fundamentals of inventory, and optimize inventory levels across financial, service, and operational perspectives. The book and its underlying RightStock™ model present a proven, fact-based, balanced, and logical means of determining the proper role and level of inventory in supply chain strategy.

Chapter 2 is devoted to inventory fundamentals, Inventory 101 if you will. I am often aghast at the misunderstanding and misapplication of inventory fundamentals. I included those fundamentals to establish a foundation for understanding more advanced inventory interdependencies within a supply chain, within the company, and with other companies. Inventory fundamentals covers (1) Inventory Integrity, (2) Inventory Philosophies, (3) Inventory Types, (4) Out of Stock Conditions, (5) Planning Parameters, (6) Financial Terms, (7) Demand Terms, (8) Decision Variables, and (9) Inventory Interdependencies.

Chapter 3 teaches our RightStock™ methodology for optimizing inventory levels, Inventory 201. The model moves progressively through the seven steps of optimizing (1) SKU portfolios, (2) forecast accuracy, (3) leadtimes, (4) lot sizes, (5) deployment, (6) visibility, and (7) inventory carrying rates.

Chapter 4 presents the role of inventory in supply chain strategy, Inventory 301. We begin by developing a full definition of supply chain logistics; teach the role of inventory in customer service, supply, transportation, and warehousing; and end by illustrating the role inventory should play in fully integrated supply chain strategies.

A glossary of key terms and formulas is also provided.

Chapter 2

Inventory Fundamentals

I rarely come across obstacles to inventory performance that cannot be overcome with fundamentals. These building blocks and intrinsic tradeoffs seem to elude all but the world-class few who have ironically recognized that **breakthroughs are in the basics**.

A few months ago I facilitated an inventory strategy workshop with a manufacturer of high tech components. During the workshop they proudly presented their supply chain and inventory performance and practices. They had even set their S&OP process set to music. Despite their advances, something was missing.

I asked if they knew their inventory data accuracies. They did not. I asked if they knew what their safety stock, lot size, and pipeline inventory levels should be. They did not. I asked if their inventory planners were certified in inventory planning. They were not. Finally, their Chief Supply Chain Officer interrupted and said, "Dr. Frazelle, are you suggesting that we need to go back to basics?" I said, "Yes, that's exactly what I'm suggesting. No strategy is sophisticated enough to survive a faulty foundation. In fact, the most successful strategies focus on fundamentals."

Our sometimes tedious journey through inventory fundamentals will take us through nine aspects of inventory fundamentals – (1) Inventory Integrity, (2) Inventory Philosophies, (3) Inventory Types, (4) Out of Stock Conditions, (5) Planning Parameters, (6) Financial Terms, (7) Demand

Terms, (8) Decision Variables, and (9) Inventory Interdependencies. We begin with integrity, the foundation of the fundamentals.

2.1 Inventory Integrity

In a recent project with one of the world's largest and most critical healthcare providers I was stunned to learn that they *did not even measure inventory accuracy*, let alone know what it was or have on-going efforts to improve it. On a project with a prestigious industrial conglomerate I helped them uncover the fact that *over 50% of their MRP and BOM data was just plain wrong*. In a project with a global aerospace company we discovered that over 500 people, some with minimal credential requirements could make multi-million dollar changes to high level production schedules with little to no oversight. In a project with a major high tech equipment company we found that unqualified inventory "analysts" were "tweaking" major inventory set points and true demand in their service parts inventory system. The pre-meditated tweaks were un-vetted, un-supervised and made to guarantee that reported turns coincided with their personal turn targets. In a recent project with one of the world's largest commodities companies the company balked at my suggestion that they even consider using the word "integrity" in reference to inventory because "integrity" sounded moral. In each case, the companies yearned for and nearly demanded the most sophisticated practices in inventory

RightChain™

management, while struggling with, ignoring, flying in the face of, and/or naively overlooking the basis for all inventory improvements – integrity.

Integrity is the foundation for everything related to trust. Trust is the fertile cultural and technical soil required for true inventory optimization. Without it, each element of the supply chain hunkers down into their own inventory protection mode, commonly known as hoarding.

High levels of inventory integrity develop from high levels of inventory accuracy; reliable base data including leadtimes, MRP records and BOM records; measured and persistently improved forecast accuracy; and consistent, disciplined participation, follow-through, and accountability by key players in inventory decision making meetings and processes.

Once a high level of **inventory integrity** is established, the next phases of inventory management maturity are attainable (Figure 2.1). Level 2 is **inventory stability**, where predictable cause and effect outcomes are the rule as opposed to the exception in inventory behavior. Level 3 is **inventory optimization**, where the SKU portfolio, forecast, leadtimes, lot sizes, deployment, visibility, inventory carrying rate, inventory turn rate, and fill rate that meet required service levels and maximize financial performance are determined and implemented. Level 4 is **inventory integration**, where inventory optimization incorporates cross-functional participation in and accountability for inventory decision making. Level 5 is **inventory collaboration,** where sharing inventory levels, forecasts, and planning with key suppliers and customers is commonplace.

Figure 2.1 Inventory Management Maturity Phases

2.2 Inventory Philosophies: Push or Pull?

There are two basic inventory management philosophies – push and pull. The push inventory model is so called because the emphasis is on "pushing" speculative inventory, made-to-stock (MTS) in response to forecasted demand, out the door to customers. The push model financially outperforms the pull model when manufacturing utilization is critical and the cost of production is high relative to inventory carrying cost and to the risk of obsolescence. We recently helped convert a variety of clients in the CPG, food, beverage, and confectioners industries to push models resulting in much higher profits, increased return on invested capital, larger market share, and improved customer satisfaction.

The pull inventory model is so called because true demand is said to "pull" made-to-order (MTO) inventory to customers on a just-in-time basis. The pull model financially outperforms the push model when the cost of inventory carrying cost and risk of obsolescence are high relative to production and postponement costs. Products such as high-end, highly configurable electronics and pharmaceuticals are examples of products that work best financially and operationally in pull-based systems.

Many demonstrative proponents of pull-based inventory and supply chain management have published and soap-boxed to the point where any other approach to inventory or supply chain management is considered second-class, immature, or old fashioned. However, in many respects pull-based programs – Lean, JIT, TPS – are philosophies founded in the highly unique logistics, business, geographical, historical, and cultural setting that is Japan. We work with clients around the world in diverse economic, competitive, geographical, and cultural settings. We compute return on invested capital, profitability, and customer satisfaction for each of their SKUs and unique nodes and links in their supply chains. We find that an *optimal mix of push and pull* depending upon product characteristics, business conditions, and transition points within the supply chain yields dramatically superior financial and service performance to strictly pull-based programs.

That optimal mix of push and pull is another facet of our RightStock™ inventory model. That optimal mix is based on a wide variety of item characteristics including demand variability, item value, shelf life, and risk of obsolescence AND logistics characteristics including setup/PO costs and inventory carrying rates. A qualitative presentation of those factors and their impact on push-pull models is presented in Figure 2.2.

Item Characteristics	Push/MTS	Pull/MTO
Shelf Life	High	Low
Setup or PO Cost	High	Low
Demand Variability	Low	High
Risk of Obsolescence	Low	High
Inventory Carrying Rate	Low	High
Item Value	Low	High

Figure 2.2 Push-Pull Decision Factors

2.3 Inventory Types

Not all inventory is created equal. Yet, when addressing inventory concerns, most companies lump all inventory into one bucket, as if it was all there for the same reason. In reality, there are different types of inventory fulfilling different roles in supply chains and business. In this section we define those unique roles

RightChain™

and the types of inventory that accompany them. We begin with
Buckets of Inventory.

2.3.1   Buckets of Inventory

A few years ago I received a phone call from one of the
world's largest CPG firms operating one of the most advanced
supply chains. They requested our assistance with inventory
strategy. I was quite surprised by the call because the firm is
widely known for its excellence in inventory management. I
expressed my surprise and curiosity and asked them why they
reached out to us. They shared that in their research of inventory
models the RightStock™ model was one of the very few that
incorporated **buckets of inventory** (BOI) as their model did.
They wanted to benchmark and utilize our model.

I asked what they meant by buckets of inventory. They
explained that they allocate inventory into three buckets – safety
stock inventory (SSI), lot size inventory (LSI), and pipeline
inventory (PI). They wanted to see if our RightStock™ model
recommended the same inventory allocations as their model. I
was encouraged by the call because the large majority of
organizations lump all inventory into one bucket, yet ***all
inventory is not the same***; it does not all serve the same
purpose.

Safety stock inventory (SSI) is required because demand
is not perfectly predictable and supplier performance is not
perfectly reliable. Lot size inventory (LSI) is necessary because

there are manufacturing economies of scale related to production run lengths and procurement economies of scale related to purchase quantities. Pipeline inventory (PI) refers to inventory that is fiscally on the books but is not physically available to sell.

To the extent we can allocate inventory into those buckets we can develop cause and effect models for each type of inventory. (To the extent we can't; inventory management becomes a trial and error guessing game.) For example, we can optimize safety stock inventory by trading off the cost of improving forecast accuracy and supplier reliability with the costs of implementing the processes and systems required to do so. An example safety stock optimization for a large aerospace company is illustrated in Figure 2.3. Note that safety stock levels are consistently too high for nearly all SKUs, in this case reflecting a strong upward bias in the forecasting process (Figure 2.4). By correcting the forecasting bias and optimizing the safety stock inventory we were able to reduce the inventory investment by 30%, over $4,000,000, and improve service levels at the same time.

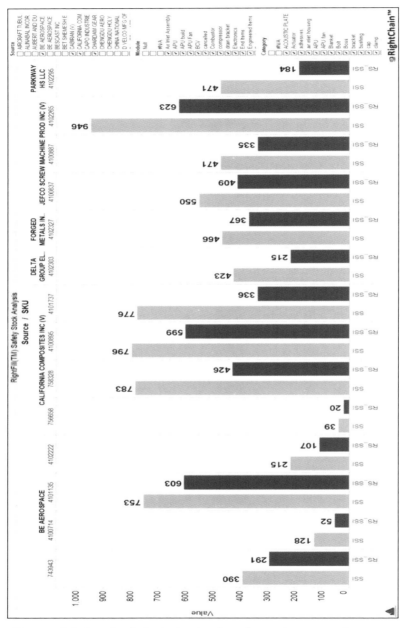

Figure 2.3 Safety Stock Optimization for a Large Aerospace Company.
RS = RightStock™, SSI = Safety Stock Inventory

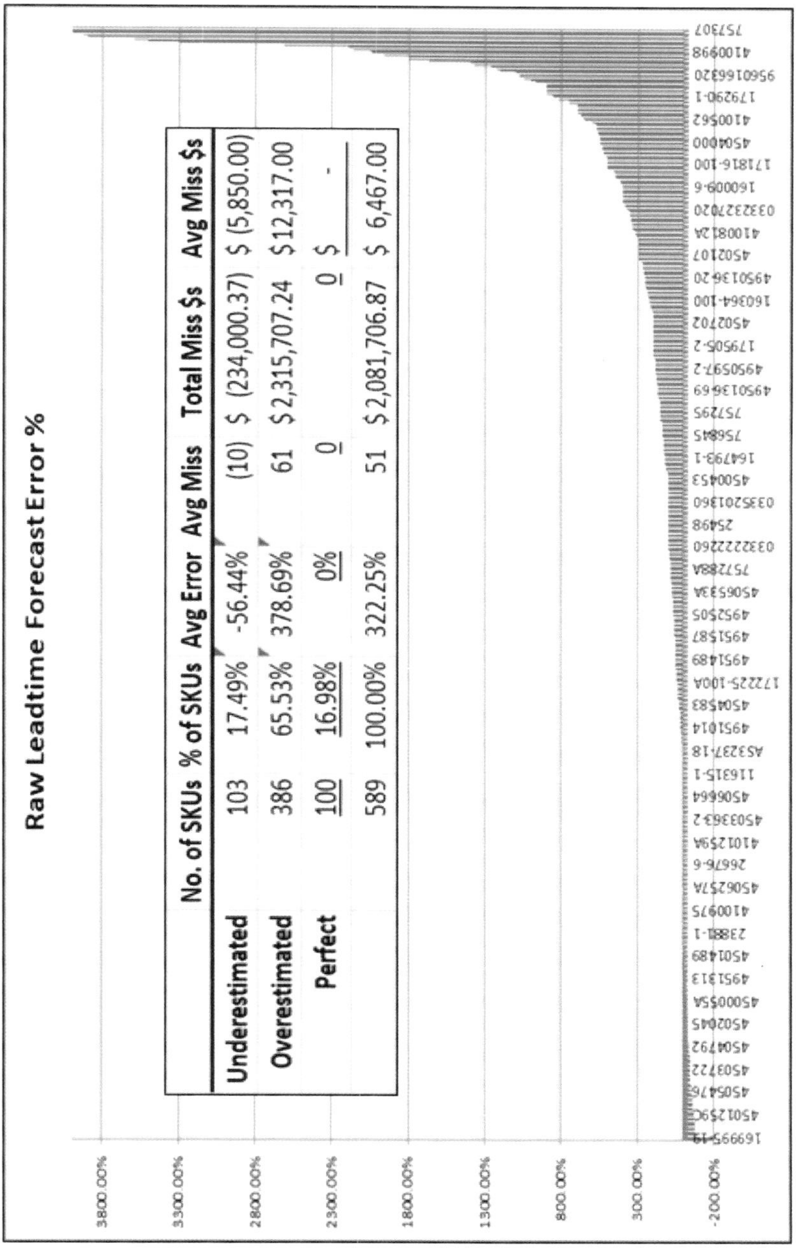

	No. of SKUs	% of SKUs	Avg Error	Avg Miss	Total Miss $s	Avg Miss $s
Underestimated	103	17.49%	-56.44%	(10)	$ (234,000.37)	$ (5,850.00)
Overestimated	386	65.53%	378.69%	61	$ 2,315,707.24	$12,317.00
Perfect	100	16.98%	0%	0	0	$ -
	589	100.00%	322.25%	51	$ 2,081,706.87	$ 6,467.00

Figure 2.4 RightCast™ Forecast Bias Analysis.
The majority (65%) of SKUs are overestimated and by a large % (379%).

RightChain™

Lot size inventories can be optimized by trading off reductions in manufacturing setup times and ordering costs with the investments required to do so. An example lot size optimization for a large bottler is illustrated in Figure 2.5. Note that their lot sizes are consistently too small. The small lot sizes reflect their overly aggressive move into lean manufacturing and their SKU proliferation which cut sharply into manufacturing capacity. Contracting the SKU base and increasing lot sizes yielded a 15% reduction in total supply chain cost, adding over $29 million per year to their bottom line.

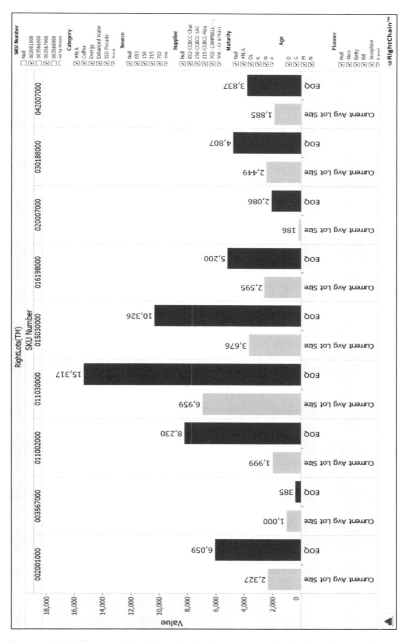

Figure 2.5 RightLots™ Lot Size Optimization Analysis for a Large Bottler

🍥RightChain™

The RightStock™ model also distinguishes between value added inventory (VAI) and excess, non-value added inventory (NVAI). Value added inventory is the sum of safety stock, lot size, and pipeline inventory. Those three types of inventory are theoretically adding value by mitigating risk in demand and supply variability, producing economies of scale in production and/or procurement, and floating fiscally and/or physically for an optimal time period before becoming on-hand inventory.

$$VAI = SSI + LSI + PI$$

Inventory not adding value in those three buckets is non-value added inventory (NVAI) - the difference between the **total inventory level** (TIL) and the value added inventory (VAI).

$$NVAI = TIL - VAI$$

Another key deliverable in our RightStock™ diagnostic is a comparative illustration of how a client's inventory should be allocated to RightStock™ buckets of inventory and the excess that remains. An example non-value added inventory diagnostic for a single SKU from a heavy industry client is illustrated in Figure 2.6. The analysis reveals non-value added inventory in units, dollars and days. In this particular case there are 393 units, $2,357.41, and 26.20 days of excess inventory. 22% of the inventory investment is excessive. This is not an atypical finding in RightStock™ assessments. Particularly disturbing is the $2,399.40 on order for an SKU that already has 22% too much inventory.

For this particular client we found that the large majority of SKUs were in a similarly over-invested state. They had large on-order quantities for even the most over-invested SKUs. Simply stopping and/or slowing down inbound orders for over-invested SKUs saved the company more than $14,000,000.

Buckets	Units	$s	Days
Safety Stock Inventory	483	$ 2,897.28	32.20
Lot Size Inventory	677	$ 4,060.98	45.13
Pipeline Inventory	249	$ 1,493.63	16.60
Value Added Inventory	1,409	$ 8,451.89	93.93
Excess Inventory	*393*	*$ 2,357.41*	*26.20*
TOTAL INVENTORY	1,802	$ 10,809.30	120.13
On Order	400	$ 2,399.40	26.67

Figure 2.6 RightStock™ Buckets of Inventory Analysis for an HVAC SKU

A similar analysis is illustrated in Figure 2.7. The figure is from a recent client in the aerospace industry and shows for each supplier the number of part numbers and the specific part numbers with excess inventory and the amount of the excess. We use this profile to work collaboratively and consistently with suppliers to identify root causes for the excess and to eliminate/minimize those excesses. In this particular case, we eliminated more than $12 million of excess inventory and maintained or improved service levels across the SKU and customer base.

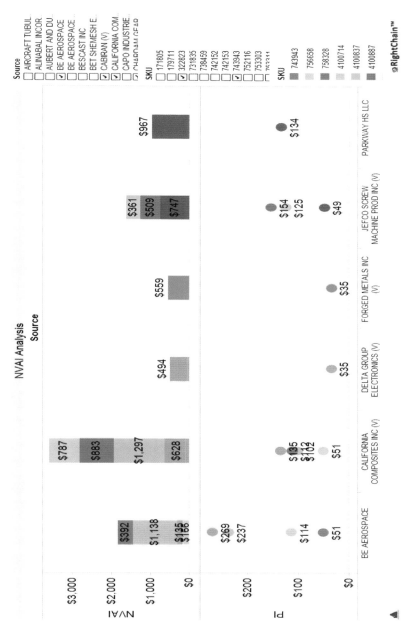

Figure 2.7 RightStock™ Excess Inventory Analysis
NVAI = Non-Value Added Inventory, PI = Pipeline Inventory

⊛RightChain™

Root Cause Analysis

We frequently find it helpful to identify and rank order root and systemic causes of excess inventory. An example completed for a large HVAC client is depicted in Figure 2.8. In this case the root causes in rank order are:

- large order releases required by Chinese suppliers (33.9% = $1,210,864),
- mis-sized purchased orders with other suppliers (31.5% = $1,126,000),
- MRP data errors (11.2% = $401,000),
- poorly negotiated minimum order quantities (4.93% = $176,319), etc.

The RightStock™ Root Cause Analysis gave birth to an extensive project plan aimed at eliminating non-value added inventory. The plan is presented in Figure 2.9. Not every plan works, but this one led to the plant being named one of America's Ten Best Plants by *Industry Week*. The plan moves through four major phases – stabilization, optimization, automation, and collaboration. The entire plan yielded an inventory reduction in excess of $7 million; a reduction in days-on-hand from 35 to 21; and an increase in on-time delivery performance from 93.5% to 97.5%.

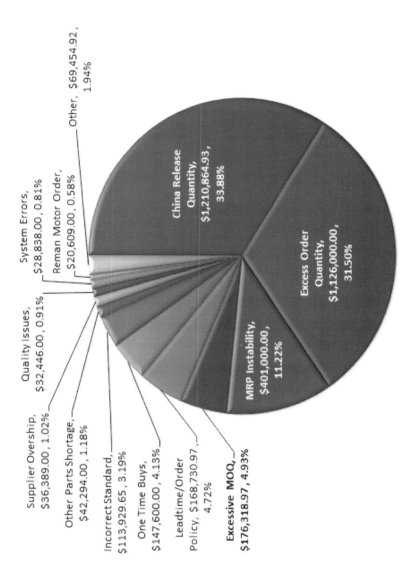

Figure 2.8 Excess Inventory Causes and Pareto for a HVAC Company

RightChain™

Initiative	Month 1	Month 2	Month 3	Month 4	Month 5	Month 6	Month 7	Month 8	Month 9	Month 10	Month 11	Month 12	PROJECTED SAVINGS ($000s)	Phase Savings ($000s)
Order Stop on High DOH		$ 250	$ 200	$ 150									$ 600	
MRP Checks & Balances		$ 250	$ 200	$ 150	$ 100								$ 700	
China Buy Quantities		$ 150	$ 200	$ 150	$ 100								$ 650	
Renegotiate MOQs		$ 40	$ 50	$ 50	$ 10	$ 50							$ 156	
Short Firm Fence		$ 10	$ 10	$ 10	$ 10	$ 6							$ 40	$ 2,146
Leadtime/Pipeline Optimization				$ 75	$ 100	$ 150	$ 100	$ 50	$ 50				$ 525	
Lot Size Optimization					$ 200	$ 250	$ 200	$ 150					$ 800	
Forecast Optimization					$ 100	$ 125	$ 100	$ 75					$ 400	
Safety Stock Optimization					$ 150	$ 200	$ 250	$ 200	$ 150				$ 950	$ 2,675
Develop & Implement MPS						$ 100	$ 100	$ 100	$ 100	$ 50			$ 450	
Implement Real-Time Inventory							$ 100	$ 150	$ 100	$ 50	$ 50		$ 450	$ 900
Customer & Supplier Collaboration							$ 50	$ 100	$ 150	$ 100	$ 50		$ 450	$ 450
PROJECTED SAVINGS	$ -	$ 700	$ 660	$ 585	$ 770	$ 881	$ 900	$ 825	$ 550	$ 200	$ 100	$ -	$ 6,171	$ 6,171
CUMULATIVE SAVINGS	$ -	$ 700	$ 1,360	$ 1,945	$ 2,715	$ 3,596	$ 4,496	$ 5,321	$ 5,871	$ 6,071	$ 6,171	$ 6,171		
Projected Ending Inventory	$14,200	$13,500	$12,840	$12,255	$11,485	$10,604	$ 9,704	$ 8,879	$ 8,329	$ 8,129	$ 8,029	$ 8,029		
Projected DOH	35.50	33.75	32.10	30.64	28.71	26.51	24.26	22.20	20.82	20.32	20.07	20.07		
Projected TURN	8.45	8.89	9.35	9.79	10.45	11.32	12.37	13.52	14.41	14.76	14.95	14.95		
Inventory Accuracy	37.5%	37.5%	42.0%	44.0%	48.0%	52.0%	55.0%	66.0%	75.0%	85.0%	90.0%	95.0%		
On-Time Delivery	93.5%	93.5%	93.5%	93.5%	94.0%	94.5%	95.0%	95.5%	96.0%	96.5%	97.0%	97.5%		

Figure 2.9 RightStock™ Project Plan for a Large HVAC Company

2.3.2 Stage Types

Inventory should also be classified by its stage in the value stream. **Raw material inventory** (RMI) has no value added. **Work-in-process** (WIP) has some value added, but is not finished. **Finished goods inventory** (FGI) has all the value that is going to be added. Just as the allocation of inventory should be optimized across buckets of safety stock, lot size, and pipeline inventory; the allocation of inventory to raw material, work-in-process, and finished goods inventory should also be optimized. To reduce inventory carrying costs, the allocation of total inventory value typically leans toward raw material inventory. However, supplier, production, and customer response leadtimes and variabilities may dictate that a higher percentage of the inventory be allocated to work-in-process and finished goods inventory. Tax structures and the transition differentials may also dictate a different allocation of inventory value across the stages.

An example inventory stage optimization for a large, high-tech manufacturing client is depicted in Figure 2.10. Note in the example that raw material inventory is consistently too high (32% higher than optimal for the highlighted commodities); work-in-process is consistently too low (17% lower than optimal for the highlighted commodities); and finished goods inventory is consistently optimal. In this case the firm had placed a great emphasis on optimizing finished goods inventory, but needed to shift their investment in raw materials to WIP to optimize

ⓢRightChain™

financial and service performance. Doing so yielded a 12% increase in Inventory Value Added™ and a 5% increase in on-time delivery.

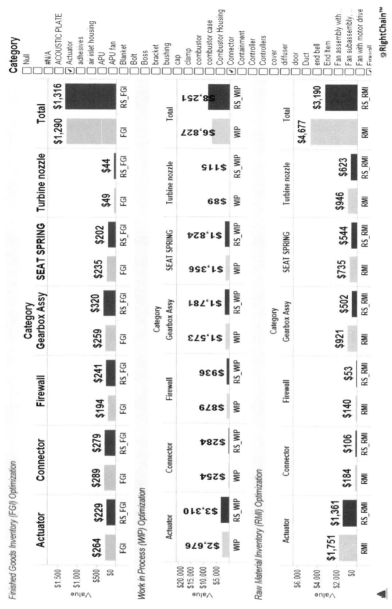

Figure 2.10 Inventory Stage Optimization for an Engine Manufacturer (RMI = Raw Material Inventory, WIP = Work-in-Process, FGI = Finished Goods Inventory, RS = RightStock™)

🐝RightChain™

2.3.2   Exceptional Types

Our RightStock™ model acknowledges seven special types of inventory: (1) Contingency & Disaster Inventory (CDI), (2) Hedge Inventory (HI), (3) Seasonality & Build Inventory (SBI), (4) Efficient Procurement Inventory (EPI), (5) Consignment Inventory, (6) Active vs. Dead Stock, and (7) Life Cycle Inventory (LCI).

Contingency and Disaster Inventory

Contingency and disaster inventory (CDI) insures against unexpected situations outside the realm of those covered by traditional safety stock inventory. Those situations include natural disasters, labor strikes, and other abnormal supply chain disruptions. For example, in our work with telecommunications and utilities clients we often plan for contingency and disaster inventory to maintain service in the event of hurricanes, floods, or snow storms.

Prophesied by Christ as the labor pains of the end times, the frequency and severity of highly unusual supply chain disruptions are increasing (Figure 2.11). In fact, according to the UN disaster risk reduction agency, UNISDR, 2011 was the most catastrophic year on record with 27,782 people killed in 302 incidents inflicting damage in excess of $366 billion. The most dramatic of those incidents was the simultaneous earthquake and tsunami that struck Japan, a place and people near and dear to my heart. Our small office in downtown Tokyo was damaged by the earthquake and one of our LogOS team members lost a relative in the tsunami. It is ironic that the incident exposing many of the risks in lean thinking would strike Japan, the birthplace of lean thinking. That incident is now the catalyst for re-thinking inventory levels and supply chains that are designed with dangerously naïve assumptions of supply chain certainties.

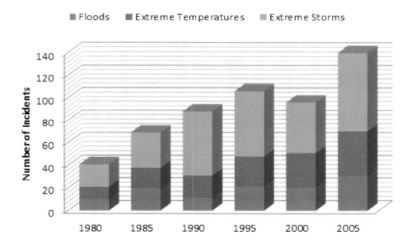

Figure 2.11 Rate of Increase in Catastrophic Incidents (Source: CRED)

Hedge Inventory

Hedge inventory (HDI) mitigates risks of potential sharp price increases, shortages in critical commodities, and extreme price and availability volatility for those same items. Fuel is a classic example of a commodity whose inventory may include a hedge inventory component.

RightChain™

Seasonality and Build Inventory

Seasonality and build inventory (SBI) levels production, machine, line and plant utilization. One of our clients is a large frozen food manufacturer and one of the world's largest producers of frozen pies. The large majority of those pies are purchased by consumers between Thanksgiving and Christmas; a short 30 day window. The demand rate then is so much greater than the demand rate during the remaining 335 days of the year that to match manufacturing capacity to demand during those days would render manufacturing virtually idle for eleven months of the year. Instead, the company produces pies at a fairly even rate during the year and stores the "build" inventory for the season in large, third-party frozen food warehouses. An example build plan is illustrated in Figure 2.12.

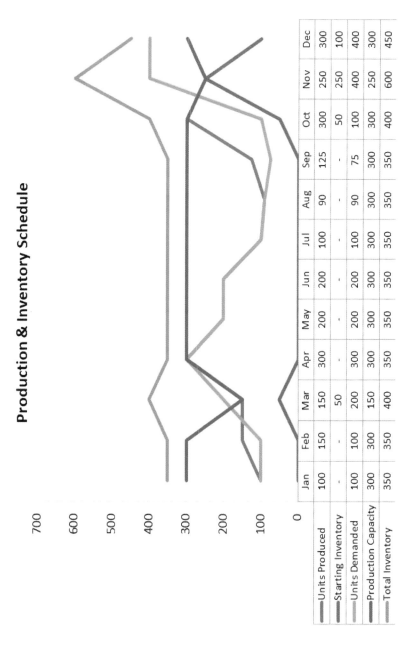

Production & Inventory Schedule

	Jan	Feb	Mar	Apr	May	Jun	Jul	Aug	Sep	Oct	Nov	Dec
Units Produced	100	150	150	300	200	200	100	90	125	300	250	300
Starting Inventory	-	-	50	-	-	-	-	-	-	50	250	100
Units Demanded	100	100	200	300	200	200	100	90	75	100	400	400
Production Capacity	300	300	150	300	300	300	300	300	300	300	250	300
Total Inventory	350	350	400	350	350	350	350	350	350	400	600	450

Figure 2.12 Seasonal/Build Inventory Example for Frozen Food

RightChain™

Efficient Procurement Inventory

Efficient procurement inventory (EPI) is often required to realize steep discounts when a special opportunity to procure arises yet requires a large purchase quantity to negotiate the deal. One of our clients is a large confectioners company. The main raw materials for their chocolate candy are sugar and cocoa. Using highly advanced weather forecasting systems and highly technical analysis of sugar and cocoa futures prices our client picks the optimal price point and time to buy mega quantities of both ingredients. Those mega quantities are housed in large storage facilities and are fairly quickly consumed in production. Since the shelf life for chocolate candy is fairly long and the risk of obsolescence is fairly low, those large buys and conversions are their most profitable inventory and supply chain strategy.

Consignment Inventory

Consignment inventory (CSI) is physically on our premises but not fiscally on our books. It is still owned by and sometimes managed by the vendor. Hence, this inventory is sometimes referred to as **vendor managed inventory** (VMI). One of our large computer clients has their entire supply base own and manage component inventory until it is picked from flow racks along their assembly line. When components are retrieved from the flow racks they become our client's property. One of our mining clients houses large quantities of service parts maintenance inventory owned by the vendor up until the point it is picked by our client and placed on a machine under repair.

Active and Dead Stock

Active and dead stock inventories are relative references to inventory that is fast vs slow/not moving. The definitions of "fast, "slow" and "not" are also relative. The most common definition of *active inventory is inventory on-hand for SKUs incurring demand within the previous twelve months.* The percentage of total inventory investment in active SKUs is the **inventory quality ratio** (IQR). IQR is a revealing indicator of inventory performance, acting akin to a bad debt ratio for banks.

An inactive inventory analysis for a recent mining client is illustrated in Figure 2.13. Note that the total inactive inventory investment has remained relatively constant over the last three years. Alarming was the growth in the number of inactive SKUs and the growth in the investment in inventory that has been inactive for 48 months. Those profiles highlighted ineffective processes that were (1) not purging inactive inventory on a regular basis, (2) allowing inactive SKUs to grow at a high rate, and (3) permitting inactivity to propagate. Once interventions were put in place, we were able to reduce investments in inactive inventory by more than $2,500,000.

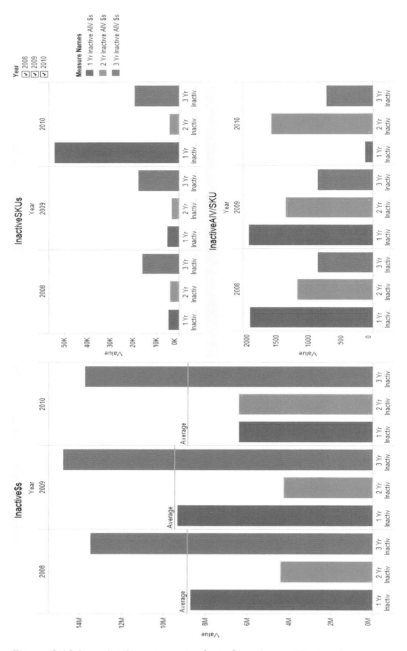

Figure 2.13 Inactive Inventory Analysis for a Large Mining Company

Life Cycle Inventory

Life Cycle Inventory (LCI) models allocate inventory to categories based on product maturities. Typical maturities include (1) Conception, (2) Infancy, (3) Adolescence, (4) Mature, (5) Aging, (6) Decline, and (7) Discontinue. An example inventory maturity curve is depicted in Figure 2.14. Just as inventory should be optimally allocated to buckets and status types; inventory should also be optimally allocated by maturity.

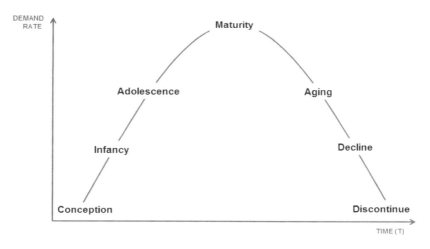

Figure 2.14 Typical Part Life Cycle Transition Curve

An example life cycle inventory optimization recently developed for a CPG client is illustrated in Figures 2.15 and 2.16. Figure 2.15 is a Life Cycle Inventory Profile. The figure highlights that the client has done an excellent job managing the number of SKUs in each phase of maturity. Figure 2.16 highlights that the

RightChain™

client is under invested in the infancy, adolescent, and mature categories.

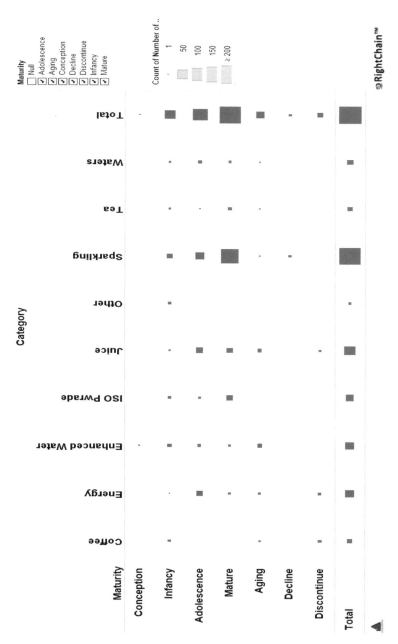

Figure 2.15 RightLife™ Inventory Profile for a Large CPG

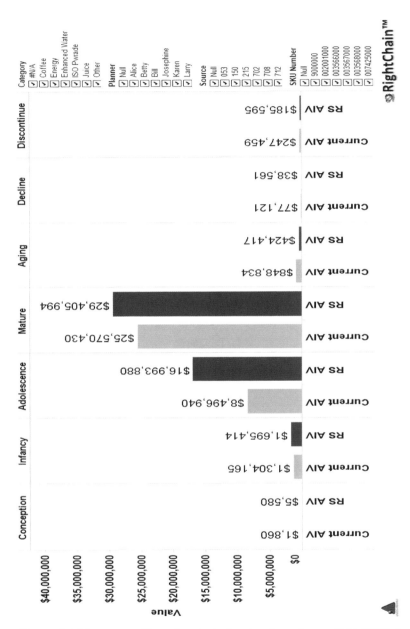

Figure 2.16 Inventory Maturity Optimization for a Large CPG ($000s)
AIV = Average Inventory Value, RS = RightStock™

2.4 Out of Stock Conditions

Never being **out of stock** (OOS) is like having an insurance policy with no deductible. The inventory carrying cost for never being out of stock is infinite, literally. As a result, not all demand can or should be satisfied directly from the shelf or sometimes at all. However, since stockouts are sometimes extremely costly in terms of lost sales, lost customer goodwill, and logistics, managing unsatisfied demand is a critical aspect of inventory management and a game changing competitive differentiator.

There are three alternative responses to unsatisfied demand - backordering, substitutions, and lost sales. The appropriate response depends on the unique price, cost, margin, and logistics characteristics of each item, customer, and channel.

In **backordering** the unfilled quantity requested by the customer is placed on a separate order called a backorder. The special "back" order is filled as soon as product is available from internal and/or external sources. In some cases the backorder is shipped directly from its original source to the customer. Backordering is commonplace when there is no other source for product (i.e. in captive markets).

Substitutions occur when a product acceptable to the customer is substituted for the product that is not available.

Lost sales occur when unsatisfied demand is lost. Lost sales are common in retail situations where there are many alternative outlets for a product. Lost sales are critically

⊛RightChain™

expensive for A+ and A items. For those items unsatisfied demand may result in negative publicity and/or the loss of customers' purchase of B or C items that depend on the availability of A items. Lost sales for B and C items, especially to B and C customers, are typically not as critical or costly.

The difference in penalties for shortages in A, B, and C items is reflected in the **shortage factor** (SF). The shortage factor is an index applied to the selling price to reflect the magnitude of the damage or "cost" of a lost sale. We define it more specifically as *the percentage of the unit selling price (USP) lost when inventory is not available*. We typically set the default value for the shortage factor at the unit gross margin percent. However, shortages of highly critical, core, or heavily promoted items may generate such negative customer reaction that customers begin to complain publicly about shortages. In those cases shortage factors may be as high as 200% to 300%. When there are readily substitutable products and competition is weak, shortage factors may be minimal.

2.5 Planning Parameters

The RightStock™ model employs six key planning parameters to define the unique inventory management characteristics for an item or enterprise –

   ▥ Unit Selling Price (USP),
   ▥ Unit Inventory Value (UIV),

- Unit Gross Margin (UGM),
- Inventory Carrying Rate (ICR),
- Purchase Order Cost (POC), and
- Setup Cost (SUC).

The **unit selling price** (USP) for an item is the price paid per unit by a customer for the item. The **unit inventory value** (UIV) for a purchased item is the price paid to the supplier for the item including inbound transportation cost. The **unit inventory value** (UIV) for a manufactured item is the cost of manufacturing the item, sometimes referred to as the standard cost. **Unit gross margin** (UGM) is the difference between unit selling price and unit inventory value. The higher the unit gross margin, the higher the cost of lost sales associated with that particular item.

$$UGM = USP - UIV$$

For example, if an item sells for $25.00 per unit and its unit inventory value is $14.00 per unit, then its unit gross margin is

$$UGM = \$25.00 - \$14.00 = \$11.00 \text{ per unit}$$

The unit gross margin percentage (UGM%) is the ratio of the unit gross margin to the unit selling price.

RightChain™

$$UGM \% = UGM/USP$$

In this case the unit gross margin percent would be

$$UGM\% = UGM/USP = \$11.00/\$25.00 = 44\%$$

The **inventory carrying rate** (ICR) is the percent of the unit inventory value used to compute **inventory carrying cost** (ICC). The inventory carrying rate includes:

- Opportunity cost of capital (the rate of return that could reasonably be achieved for each dollar not invested in inventory);
- Storage and material handling;
- Loss due to obsolescence, mark downs, damage, and/or pilferage; and
- Insurance and taxes.

Inventory carrying rates vary widely across geographies and industries. When we work in Latin American countries interest rates may be as high as 60% per year. As a result, inventory carrying rates may be as high as 70% or 80%. When we work in Japan, where interest rates are low, inventory carrying rates are much lower; perhaps in the range of 5% to 15%. When we work in the Silicon Valley, where expectations for capital investments are upwards of 20% per year, the inventory carrying rate is normally around 40%. When we work in mature industries in the mid-west, inventory carrying rates are typically between 25% and 35%. When we work with clients in the frozen food industry inventory carrying rates are typically higher due to the high cost of frozen and refrigerated storage space.

Due to the wide variety of interest rates and storage conditions, each company should determine, maintain, and publish its own inventory carrying rate. The most advanced supply chain organizations compute and maintain inventory carrying rates uniquely for each SKU.

The **purchase order cost** (POC) is the cost of placing a purchase order from a vendor. The majority of those costs are related to sourcing, purchasing, and procurement salaries and benefits (*italics*) and include:

- *Purchase Order Planning*
- *Purchase Order Entry Time*
- *Purchase Order Processing Time*
- *Purchase Order Inspection Time*
- *Purchase Order Follow-up Time*
- *Purchasing Management*
- *Authorization*
- *Tracking and Expediting*
- *Inbound Transportation, Receiving and Inspection*
- Order Forms
- Postage
- Telecommunications
- Office Space
- Office Supplies
- Purchase Order Entry Systems

RightChain™

Based on making these computations in many industries, in many geographies, over many years; the cost of placing a purchase order typically ranges between $100.00 and $500.00. The most expensive activities are *labor related activities*. Hence, automating purchase order planning and processing typically yields significant labor cost reductions and productivity improvements. In addition, blanket purchase orders; vendor managed inventories; joint, fixed cycle replenishments; supplier rationalization and integration; e-procurement; and on-premise supplier programs should be evaluated to optimize purchase order costs and their related lot sizes.

Setup cost (SUC) is the cost to setup (prepare or changeover) a machine or production line to make a production run for a particular item or change between items. It is sometimes referred to as **changeover cost** (COC). Setup or changeover costs include:

- Labor to prepare for and execute the changeover.
- Training of typically highly skilled labor.
- Lost production capacity during the changeover.
- Material lost before, during, and just after the changeover.
- Tools required for executing high-speed changeovers.
- Computer hardware and software to plan and execute changeovers.

Setup costs vary more widely than purchase order costs. We have encountered setup costs with our clients ranging from $100 to $10,000 per setup. The most expensive component is normally the opportunity cost of lost production time. Parallel processing, early tool preparation, point-of-change tool placement, optimized changeover sequencing, comprehensive and repeated changeover practice sessions, dedicated lines, and focused factories techniques and investments should be evaluated to optimize setup and changeover costs and their related production lot sizes.

2.6   Financial Terms

The RightStock™ inventory optimization methodology incorporates seven key financial terms:

- Average Inventory Value (AIV)
- Gross Margin Return on Inventory (GMROI)
- Inventory Turn Rate (ITR)
- Inventory Carrying Cost (ICC)
- Lost Sales Cost (LSC)
- Inventory Policy Cost™ (IPC)
- Inventory Value Added™ (IVA)

Average Inventory Value

Average inventory value (AIV) is the average value of the total inventory investment over the course of a year. It should be computed as the average of several on-hand inventory values measured at random times during the year. An example average inventory value calculation for a major textiles company is illustrated in Figure 2.17. The average is computed by taking the average of 13 end-of-period inventory values. Though better than quarterly figures, any end of period values may be somewhat misleading due to the fact that inventory levels tend to be lowest then.

The natural assumption for average inventory value is that lower is better, especially if it is charted in isolation. However, average inventory value is properly presented relative to target values, within control limits, and/or with respect to service levels. Those presentations are required to demonstrate the critical relationship between inventory investment and the fill rate provided by that investment. Accordingly, inventory values are plotted relative to target investments required to support target service levels in Figure 2.17. Figures 2.18 and 2.19 display expected average inventory values required to support target unit fill rates ranging from 50% to 99.95%. Note that as target fill rates increase, so does the expected inventory value required to support them. In Figure 2.18 the expected average inventory for a B SKU ranges from $42,463 to $51,480 to support target fill rates ranging from 50% to 99.97%. In Figure 2.19 the expected average inventory for a C SKU ranges from $77,847 to $221,445.

The figures are SKUBoard™ screen shots from our RightStock™ Inventory Optimization System, currently being used to guide the inventory decision making in many of the world's largest and most successful supply chains. This particular example is from a large food and beverage company.

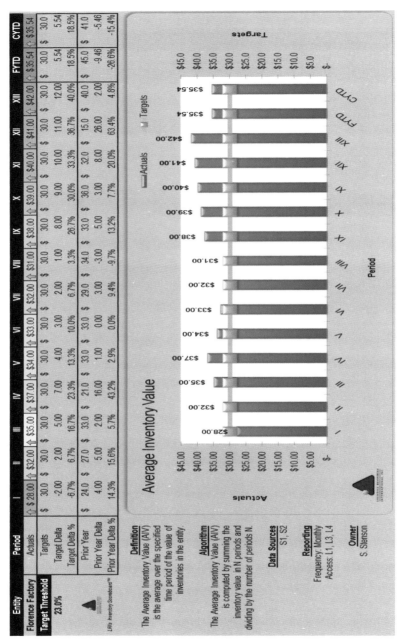

Entity	Period	I	II	III	IV	V	VI	VII	VIII	IX	X	XI	XII	XIII	FYTD	CYTD
Florence Factory	Actuals	$ 28.00	$32.00	$35.00	$37.00	$34.00	$33.00	$32.00	$31.00	$38.00	$39.00	$40.00	$41.00	$42.00	$35.54	$35.54
Target Threshold 23.0%	Targets	30.0	30.0	30.0	30.0	30.0	30.0	30.0	30.0	30.0	30.0	30.0	30.0	30.0	30.0	30.0
	Target Delta	-2.00	2.00	5.00	7.00	4.00	3.00	2.00	1.00	8.00	9.00	10.00	11.00	12.00	5.54	5.54
	Target Delta %	-6.7%	6.7%	16.7%	23.3%	13.3%	10.0%	6.7%	3.3%	26.7%	30.0%	33.3%	36.7%	40.0%	18.5%	18.5%
	Prior Year	$ 24.0	27.0	33.0	21.0	33.0	33.0	29.0	34.0	33.0	36.0	32.0	15.0	40.0	45.0	41.0
	Prior Year Delta	4.00	5.00	2.00	16.00	1.00	0.00	3.00	-3.00	5.00	3.00	8.00	26.00	2.00	-9.46	-5.46
	Prior Year Delta %	14.3%	15.6%	5.7%	43.2%	2.9%	0.0%	9.4%	-9.7%	13.2%	7.7%	20.0%	63.4%	4.8%	-26.6%	-15.4%

LRI's Inventory Scoreboard™

Definition

The Average Inventory Value (AIV) is the average over the specified time period of the value of inventories in the entity.

Algorithm

The Average Inventory Value (AIV) is computed by summing the inventory value in N periods and dividing by the number of periods N.

Data Sources
S1, S2

Reporting
Frequency: Monthly
Access: L1, L3, L4

Owner
S. Stenson

Figure 2.17 Avg. Inventory Value Computation for a Textiles Company

Parameters

SKU or Category	002001000 — 400ML SPARLST2 SW CLASSIC ORNAMENT — 961- CCE-JACKSONVILLE FLA
# of SKUs	1
Forecast Annual Demand (FAD)	106,634
Leadtime Forecast Error	9%
Unit Selling Price (USP, $/case)	10.57
Unit Inventory Value (UIV)	5.96
Shortage Factor (SF)	43.57%
Leadtime (L, Days)	14.00
Cost per Setup or PO	$ 308.00
Inventory Carrying Rate (ICR)	30%
FAD Rank Percentile	57%

LRI's SKUBoard™

Unit Fill Rate	Average Inventory Value (AIV)	Inventory Carrying Cost (ICC)	Lost Sales Cost (LSC)	Inventory Policy Cost (IPC)	Turns	Gross Margin (GM)	GMROI	Inventory Value Added (IVA)™
50.00%	$ 42,463	$ 12,739	$ 245,568	$ 258,307	15.0	$ 245,568	5.78	$ 232,829
60.00%	$ 43,128	$ 12,938	$ 196,454	$ 209,393	14.7	$ 294,681	6.83	$ 281,743
65.00%	$ 43,475	$ 13,043	$ 171,897	$ 184,940	14.6	$ 319,238	7.34	$ 306,196
70.00%	$ 43,841	$ 13,152	$ 147,341	$ 160,493	14.5	$ 343,795	7.84	$ 330,643
75.00%	$ 44,235	$ 13,270	$ 122,784	$ 136,054	14.4	$ 368,352	8.33	$ 355,081
80.00%	$ 44,674	$ 13,402	$ 98,227	$ 111,629	14.2	$ 392,908	8.79	$ 379,506
85.00%	$ 45,186	$ 13,556	$ 73,670	$ 87,226	14.1	$ 417,465	9.24	$ 403,909
90.00%	$ 45,830	$ 13,749	$ 49,114	$ 62,863	13.9	$ 442,022	9.64	$ 428,273
92.50%	$ 46,245	$ 13,874	$ 36,835	$ 50,709	13.8	$ 454,300	9.82	$ 440,427
95.00%	$ 46,785	$ 14,035	$ 24,557	$ 38,592	13.6	$ 466,579	9.97	$ 452,543
97.00%	$ 47,405	$ 14,221	$ 14,734	$ 28,955	13.4	$ 476,402	10.05	$ 462,180
98.00%	$ 47,859	$ 14,358	$ 9,823	$ 24,180	13.3	$ 481,313	10.06	$ 466,955
99.00%	$ 48,576	$ 14,573	$ 4,911	$ 19,484	13.1	$ 486,224	10.01	$ 471,652
99.50%	$ 49,231	$ 14,769	$ 2,456	$ 17,225	12.9	$ 488,680	9.93	$ 473,911
99.60%	$ 49,431	$ 14,829	$ 1,965	$ 16,794	12.9	$ 489,171	9.90	$ 474,342
99.70%	$ 49,683	$ 14,905	$ 1,473	$ 16,378	12.8	$ 489,662	9.86	$ 474,757
99.80%	$ 50,026	$ 15,008	$ 982	$ 15,990	12.7	$ 490,153	9.80	$ 475,146
99.90%	$ 50,583	$ 15,175	$ 491	$ 15,666	12.6	$ 490,644	9.70	$ 475,470
99.91%	$ 50,665	$ 15,199	$ 442	$ 15,641	12.6	$ 490,694	9.69	$ 475,494
99.93%	$ 50,857	$ 15,257	$ 344	$ 15,601	12.5	$ 490,792	9.65	$ 475,535
99.95%	$ 51,109	$ 15,333	$ 246	$ 15,578	12.4	$ 490,890	9.60	$ 475,557
99.97%	$ 51,480	$ 15,444	$ 147	$ 15,591	12.4	$ 490,988	9.54	$ 475,544

Maturity / Current

	Unit Fill Rate	AIV	ICC	LSC	IPC	Turns	GM	GMROI	IVA
Current	99.60%	$ 45,879	$ 13,764	$ 1,965	$ 15,728	13.9	$ 489,171	10.66	$ 475,407
	UGM/Cube P $ 0.0697	UGM1% 43.6%	UGM2% 34.1%	UGM3% 32.9%	UGM4% 29.1%	UGM$/Cube $ 0.047	103.5%	GMROI/Cube 0.161	IVA/Cube $ 7,198.74
Rank %	64.5%	61.5%	61.8%	63.1%	63.9%	ROIC 68.2%	81.4%	82.5%	72.0%

Figure 2.18 RightStock™ Inventory Optimization for a Food & Beverage Company – B SKU

RightChain™

LRI's SKUBoard™ — Input Parameters

SKU or Category	348560000
	1602 CAN 4PK 24 PB MONSTER ENERGY
	72 HANSEN BEVERAGE COMPANY
# of SKUs	1
Forecast Annual Demand (FAD)	20,547
Leadtime Forecast Error	55%
Unit Selling Price (USP, $/case)	30.46
Unit Inventory Value (UIV)	27.07
Shortage Factor (SF)	11.13%
Leadtime (L, Days)	40.00
Cost per Setup or PO	308.00
Inventory Carrying Rate (ICR)	30%
FAD Rank Percentile	26%
Maturity	

RightStock™ Optimization Table

Unit Fill Rate	Average Inventory Value (AIV)	Inventory Carrying Cost (ICC)	Lost Sales Cost (LSC)	Inventory Policy Cost (IPC)	Turns	Gross Margin (GM)	GMROI	Inventory Value Added (IVA)™
50.00%	$ 77,847	$ 23,354	$ 34,845	$ 58,199	7.1	$ 34,845	0.448	$ 11,491
60.00%	$ 88,449	$ 26,535	$ 27,876	$ 54,410	6.3	$ 41,814	0.473	$ 15,279
65.00%	$ 93,971	$ 28,191	$ 24,391	$ 52,583	5.9	$ 45,298	0.482	$ 17,107
70.00%	$ 99,791	$ 29,937	$ 20,907	$ 50,844	5.6	$ 48,783	0.489	$ 18,845
75.00%	$ 106,072	$ 31,821	$ 17,422	$ 49,244	5.2	$ 52,267	0.493	$ 20,446
80.00%	$ 113,065	$ 33,920	$ 13,938	$ 47,857	4.9	$ 55,752	0.493	$ 21,832
85.00%	$ 121,217	$ 36,365	$ 10,453	$ 46,819	4.6	$ 59,236	0.489	$ 22,871
90.00%	$ 131,474	$ 39,442	$ 6,969	$ 46,411	4.2	$ 62,721	0.477	$ 23,278
92.50%	$ 138,085	$ 41,426	$ 5,227	$ 46,652	4.0	$ 64,463	0.467	$ 23,037
95.00%	$ 146,677	$ 44,003	$ 3,484	$ 47,488	3.8	$ 66,205	0.451	$ 22,202
97.00%	$ 156,550	$ 46,965	$ 2,091	$ 49,056	3.6	$ 67,599	0.432	$ 20,634
98.00%	$ 163,787	$ 49,136	$ 1,394	$ 50,530	3.4	$ 68,296	0.417	$ 19,160
99.00%	$ 175,194	$ 52,558	$ 697	$ 53,255	3.2	$ 68,993	0.394	$ 16,434
99.50%	$ 185,634	$ 55,690	$ 348	$ 56,039	3.0	$ 69,341	0.374	$ 13,651
99.60%	$ 188,824	$ 56,647	$ 279	$ 56,926	2.9	$ 69,411	0.368	$ 12,764
99.70%	$ 192,829	$ 57,849	$ 209	$ 58,058	2.9	$ 69,481	0.360	$ 11,632
99.80%	$ 198,285	$ 59,486	$ 139	$ 59,625	2.8	$ 69,550	0.351	$ 10,065
99.90%	$ 207,160	$ 62,148	$ 70	$ 62,218	2.7	$ 69,620	0.336	$ 7,472
99.91%	$ 208,463	$ 62,539	$ 63	$ 62,602	2.7	$ 69,627	0.334	$ 7,088
99.93%	$ 211,529	$ 63,459	$ 49	$ 63,507	2.6	$ 69,641	0.329	$ 6,182
99.95%	$ 215,541	$ 64,662	$ 35	$ 64,697	2.6	$ 69,655	0.323	$ 4,993
99.97%	$ 221,445	$ 66,433	$ 21	$ 66,454	2.5	$ 69,669	0.315	$ 3,235
Current 99.60%	$ 35,190	$ 10,557	$ 279	$ 10,836	15.8	$ 69,411	1.97	$ 58,854

	UGM/Cube	UGM1%	UGM2%	UGM3%	UGM4%	UGM4/Cube	ROIC	GMROI/Cube	IVA/Cube
Maturity	$ 0.0182	11.1%	7.9%	6.2%	4.9%	$ 0.008	10.3%	0.011	$ 315.49
Rank %	41.6%	8.3%	9.4%	11.5%	12.9%	35.7%	20.6%	11.1%	21.2%

Figure 2.19 RightStock™ Inventory Optimization for a Food & Beverage Company – C SKU

Gross Margin Return on Inventory

Gross margin return on inventory (GMROI) is the ratio of gross margin (GM) to average inventory value. It is akin to a return on investment analysis for inventory. The metric is increasingly popular in retailing, however, it is still underutilized in that industry as well as most other industries.

$$GMROI = GM/AIV$$

GMROIs associated with fill rates ranging from 50% to 99.95% for a medium moving beverage SKU were illustrated in Figure 2.18. The example is taken from a recent inventory optimization engagement with one of the nation's largest bottling groups. The maximum GMROI is 10.06 achieved at a fill rate of 98.00% and a turn rate of 13.3. The analysis helped the client realize that in their case inventory was relatively inexpensive compared to lost sales cost and lost gross margin and led to substantial, profitable increases in inventory investments. The GMROI optimization for a slower moving, less profitable, and less forecastable SKU is in Figure 2.19. The maximum GMROI for that SKU is 0.493 achieved at a target fill rate of 75% and a target turn rate of 5.2.

In addition to GMROI, we also often recommend the use of GMROI per unit cube as a guiding metric where shelf space is limited. We used the metric to great effect in three recent engagements; stocking beverages in retail grocery and

⊛RightChain™

convenience store aisles; stocking jewelry and cosmetics in high-end retailing; and stocking frozen food items on home delivery trucks. GMROI per unit cube for an SKU is in Figure 2.18, computed as 0.161.

Inventory Turn Rate

The inventory turn rate (ITR) is most commonly expressed as the ratio of the cost of goods sold (COGS) to the average inventory value (AIV).

$$ITR = COGS/AIV$$

For example, if a company experiences cost of goods sold of $412,000,000/year and maintains an average inventory value of $83,000,000, then its inventory turn rate is:

$$ITR = \$412,000,000 \ / \ \$83,000,000 = 4.97 \text{ turns per year}$$

To differentiate it from retail and unit turns, we sometimes refer to the inventory turn rate as turns at cost (TAC). Turns at retail (TAR) is the ratio of annual sales to average inventory value.

$$TAR = Sales/AIV$$

In the example above, if that company had annual sales of $1,114,000,000 then its turns at retail would be

TAR = $1,114,000,000/$83,000,000 = 13.42 retail turns per year

Those first two ratios are fiscal inventory turn rates. Turns can also be measured physically. We refer to the physical inventory turn rate as the unit turn rate (UTR). It is the ratio of annual units shipped (AUS) to the average inventory level (AIL) in units.

$$UTR = AUS/AIL$$

For example, if a company ships 350,000 cases per year and has an average inventory level of 73,000 cases, then its unit turn rate is

$$UTR = 350,000 / 73,000 = 4.79 \text{ unit turns per year}$$

Considered in isolation, higher inventory turn rates are preferred to lower inventory turn rates. However, the inventory turn rate is a critical factor in a wide range of supply chain decisions and should be set to optimize the performance of the business and supply chain as a whole. As a result, inventory turn rates should be evaluated within control limits or relative to targets set in conjunction with fill rates and other fiscal measures of inventory performance.

RightChain™

Inventory Carrying Cost

Inventory carrying cost (ICC) annualizes the cost of carrying (or holding) the average inventory value.   The annualization is important because it allows inventory carrying cost to be placed alongside and optimized with lost sales cost, transportation cost, and warehousing cost in the computation of total supply chain costs.

Inventory carrying cost is computed by multiplying the average inventory value (AIV) by the inventory carrying rate (ICR).

$$ICC = AIV \times ICR$$

For example, if the average inventory value in a warehouse is $10,000,000 and the inventory carrying rate is 30% per year, then the inventory carrying cost in the warehouse is

$$ICC = \$10{,}000{,}000 \times 30\%/year = \$3{,}000{,}000 \text{ per year.}$$

Expected inventory carrying costs associated with target unit fill rates ranging from 50% to 99.95% for a medium moving SKU in a large food and beverage company were presented in Figure 2.18. Note that inventory carrying costs grow from a low of $12,739 per year at a target fill rate of 50% to a high of $15,444 per year at a target unit fill rate of 99.97%.

Lost Sales Cost

Lost sales cost (LSC) is the cost of the sales lost when we are not able to satisfy customer demand. The lost sales cost for an item is computed by multiplying its annual sales potential (i.e. sales that would have occurred if all demand was satisfied = AD x USP) by the portion of sales that we were not able to satisfy (1 – UFR) by the shortage factor (SF).

$$LSC = [AD \times USP] \times (1 - UFR) \times SF$$

For example, if an item has an annual demand of 2,000 units per year; a unit selling price of $2,400 per unit; a unit fill rate of 90%; and a shortage factor of 40% then the lost sales cost is

$$LSC = [2,000 \times \$2,400] \times (1 - .9) \times (.4) = [\$4,800,000] \times .1 \times .4 =$$
$$\$192,000 \text{ per year}$$

In Figure 2.18 the expected lost sales costs associated with a medium moving SKU were plotted vs. target unit fill rates and inventory investments required to achieve them. Note that expected lost sales cost declines from $245,568 per year at a target unit fill rate of 50% to $147 per year at a target unit fill rate of 99.95%.

Inventory Policy Cost

The inventory policy cost (IPC) for an item is the sum of inventory carrying cost and lost sales cost for the item. It strikes *a balance between the financial costs and benefits of inventory availability.*

$$IPC = ICC + LSC$$

One way to play the inventory game is to set unit fill rate and inventory turn rate targets to minimize inventory policy cost. Inventory policy costs for target fill rates ranging from 50% to 99.95% for two food and beverage SKUs were provided in Figures 2.18 and 2.19. The SKU in Figure 2.18 is a medium moving SKU with a low forecast error and a short leadtime. The minimum inventory policy cost is $15,578 at a target unit fill rate of 99.95% and a target turn rate of 12.4 with an associated target inventory investment of $51,109. The same computations for a slow moving SKU with a higher forecast error, longer leadtime, and smaller unit gross margin were provided in Figure 2.19. The minimum inventory policy cost for that SKU is at a target unit fill rate of 90% with a target turn rate of 4.0.

Inventory Value Added

LRI developed **Inventory Value Added™** (IVA) as an inventory financial performance measure several years ago. It is the difference between gross margin and inventory carrying cost.

Like GMROI, it **holds gross margin accountable for the inventory investment required to achieve it.** It is the best indicator we have developed so far to predict the impact of various inventory strategies on shareholder value.

$$IVA = GM - ICC$$

In the example in Figure 2.18, the maximum IVA™ is $475,557 achieved at a target unit fill rate of 99.95% and a target inventory turn rate of 12.4. For the slower moving SKU in Figure 2.19 the maximum IVA™ is $23,878 achieved at a target unit fill rate of 90.00% and a target inventory turn rate of 4.2.

Slow Moving Consumer Products

Figure 2.20 is an example inventory optimization for a large consumer products business unit. When I put the first screen shot up the president called it an eye chart and begrudgingly got up out of his chair to read it. He asked me to help him interpret the chart and to figure out the optimal target fill rate. I asked him what his main financial objective was for the coming year. He said they wanted to increase shareholder value. I shared with him that the metric most closely tied to shareholder value was Inventory Value Added™. He pointed to that column, read down the list until he came to the highest value, took his finger across to the corresponding fill rate, and said, "You mean to tell me that our target fill rate for C SKUs

RightChain™

should be 99%?" I said, "for those C SKUs, yes." He asked what
the current target was. I said, 92%. He asked me what would
happen if they raised the fill rate target. I said, "Your profit,
market share, customer satisfaction, shareholder value, and
inventory levels will increase." He turned to the head of supply
chain planning and told him to design a regional pilot to try the
strategy. The pilot lasted three months. Thankfully the
predictions came true. The company expanded the pilot
nationwide and soon thereafter won their industry's awards for
customer satisfaction and operational excellence.

Category C's	Forecast Error	Setup Cost	Lead Time	ICR	SKUs	Shortage Factor
	52.0%	$ 2,000	19	45%	32	50%

Customer Service Level	Unit Fill Rate	Average Inventory Value	Inventory Carrying Cost	Lost Sales Cost	Inventory Policy Cost	Turns	Gross Margin	GMROI	Inventory Value Added (IVA)
50%	50.00%	$ 1,888,903	$ 850,006	$ 4,737,293	$ 5,587,300	5.02	$ 4,737,293	2.51	$ 3,887,287
60%	60.00%	$ 2,005,653	$ 902,544	$ 3,789,835	$ 4,692,379	4.72	$ 5,684,752	2.83	$ 4,782,208
65%	65.00%	$ 2,066,471	$ 929,912	$ 3,316,105	$ 4,246,017	4.58	$ 6,158,481	2.98	$ 5,228,570
70%	70.00%	$ 2,130,563	$ 958,753	$ 2,842,376	$ 3,801,130	4.45	$ 6,632,211	3.11	$ 5,673,457
75%	75.00%	$ 2,199,729	$ 989,878	$ 2,368,647	$ 3,358,525	4.31	$ 7,105,940	3.23	$ 6,116,062
80%	80.00%	$ 2,276,749	$ 1,024,537	$ 1,894,917	$ 2,919,454	4.16	$ 7,579,670	3.33	$ 6,555,133
85%	85.00%	$ 2,366,524	$ 1,064,936	$ 1,421,188	$ 2,486,124	4.00	$ 8,053,399	3.40	$ 6,988,463
90%	90.00%	$ 2,479,482	$ 1,115,767	$ 947,459	$ 2,063,226	3.82	$ 8,527,128	3.44	$ 7,411,361
92.5%	92.50%	$ 2,552,285	$ 1,148,528	$ 710,594	$ 1,859,122	3.71	$ 8,763,993	3.43	$ 7,615,465
95%	95.00%	$ 2,646,903	$ 1,191,107	$ 473,729	$ 1,664,836	3.58	$ 9,000,858	3.40	$ 7,809,751
97%	97.00%	$ 2,755,632	$ 1,240,034	$ 284,238	$ 1,524,272	3.44	$ 9,190,349	3.34	$ 7,950,315
98%	98.00%	$ 2,835,335	$ 1,275,901	$ 189,492	$ 1,465,393	3.34	$ 9,285,095	3.27	$ 8,009,194
99%	99.00%	$ 2,960,958	$ 1,332,431	$ 94,746	$ 1,427,177	3.20	$ 9,379,841	3.17	$ 8,047,410
99.5%	99.50%	$ 3,075,926	$ 1,384,167	$ 47,373	$ 1,431,540	3.08	$ 9,427,214	3.06	$ 8,043,047
99.7%	99.70%	$ 3,155,167	$ 1,419,825	$ 28,424	$ 1,448,249	3.00	$ 9,446,163	2.99	$ 8,026,338
99.95%	99.95%	$ 3,405,282	$ 1,532,377	$ 4,737	$ 1,537,114	2.78	$ 9,469,850	2.78	$ 7,937,473

Figure 2.20 RightStock™ Inventory Optimization - Slow Moving CPG SKUs

☺RightChain™

2.7   Demand Terms

Every item has a unique set of demand characteristics. Some of those characteristics can be represented mathematically including -

- Annual Demand (AD),
- Forecast Annual Demand (FAD),
- Leadtime (L),
- Leadtime Demand (LD),
- Forecast Leadtime Demand (FLD),
- Standard Deviation of Leadtime Demand (SDLD), and
- Leadtime Forecast Error Percent (LFEP).

The **annual demand** (AD) for an item is the number of units requested for an item during a year. It looks backward over the prior year and is strictly historical. The **forecast annual demand** (FAD) is the forecasted (or expected) annual number of units requested by customers over the upcoming twelve months. The **leadtime** (L) for an item is the elapsed time from the placement of the replenishment order until the item is available to satisfy customer demand (Point 4 in Figure 2.21). **Leadtime demand** (LD) is the historic number of units requested by customers during a leadtime (Point 5 in Figure 2.21). The **forecast leadtime demand** (FLD) is the forecasted (or expected) number of units that will be requested by customers during a future leadtime. The expected value of the forecast leadtime demand is the product of average leadtime in days and average daily demand.

$$FLD = L \times (FAD/365)$$

For example, if an item has a leadtime of 60 days and a forecasted annual demand of 12,000 units, then its forecast leadtime demand is

$$FLD = 60 \text{ days} \times (12,000 \text{ units}/365 \text{ days}) =$$
$$60 \text{ days} \times (33 \text{ units/day}) = 1,980 \text{ units}$$

The standard deviation of leadtime demand (SDLD) is a measure of the variability of the demand during a lead time (Point 6 in Figure 2.21). The greater the variability in leadtime demand, the greater the need for safety stock to protect against large spikes in demand during a leadtime.

Leadtime forecast error percent (LFEP) is the absolute value of the forecast error over a leadtime. The greater the error, the greater the safety stock inventory required to support a given fill rate. In addition, since the forecast is used in nearly every major supply chain decision, the greater the error, the greater the error in all supply chain decision making. I can say from experience that bias and a lack of individual accountability for forecast accuracy are the two principal reasons for poor forecasting.

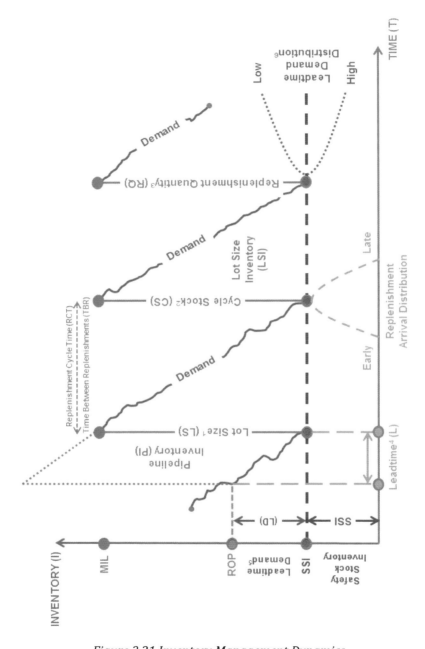

Figure 2.21 Inventory Management Dynamics

2.8 Decision Variables

The RightStock™ inventory model works to make key decisions for the following variables which work together to comprise an inventory strategy:

- Lot Size (LS)
- Unit Fill Rate (UFR)
- Safety Stock Inventory (SSI)
- Re-Order Point (ROP)
- Order-up-to-Level (OUL)
- Review Time Period (RTP)

Lot Size

The *lot size* (LS) (also known as the **replenishment quantity** (RQ) or the **cycle stock** (CS)) is the number of units that arrive in a replenishment lot or are produced in a manufacturing lot (Points 1, 2, and 3 in Figure 2.21). The **average replenishment quantity** (ARQ) is the average size of lot size replenishments derived by dividing the total replenishment quantity over a particular period of time by the number of replenishments received during that time.

Economic Order Quantity

The **economic order quantity** (EOQ) is the lot size that minimizes the sum of ordering cost and inventory carrying cost associated with the size of the order (Figure 2.22). The higher

RightChain™

the order quantity, the greater the inventory level. However, the higher the order quantity the fewer the number of orders and the lower the resulting ordering cost.

The economic run quantity (ERQ) is the production lot size (or run quantity) that minimizes the total of setup/changeover costs and the inventory carrying costs associated with the inventory produced by the run length. The tradeoffs between manufacturing setup cost and inventory carrying costs for determining optimal production run sizes for a large textiles client are illustrated in Figure 2.23. Note in the example that the optimal run length is 3 or 4 rolls per setup for that particular SKU. As is often the case with EOQ modeling, the total cost curve is fairly flat near the optimal solution. The key, as is often the key, is to make decisions that are at least in the "ballpark of optimal". Unfortunately we often find that lot sizing is off by 200% or 300%.

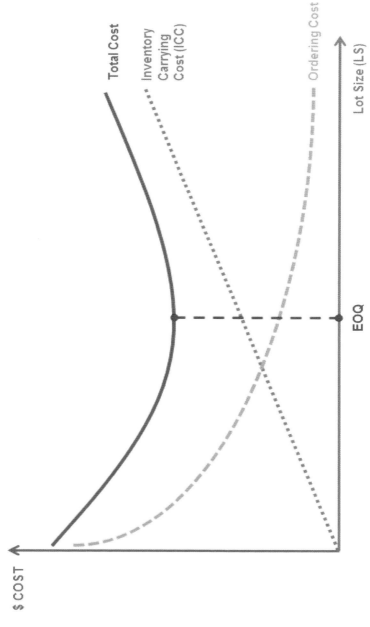

Figure 2.22 Lot Size Optimization Curve

RightChain™

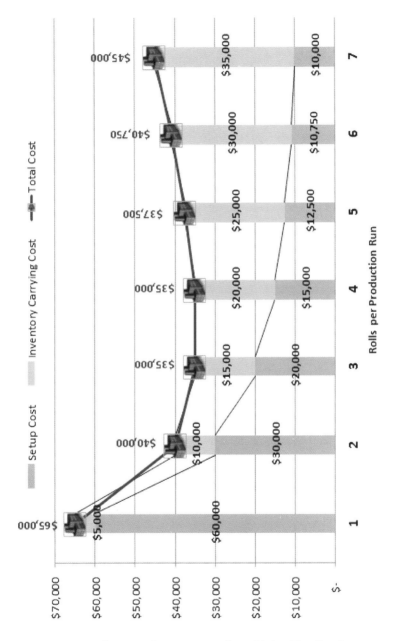

Figure 2.23 RightLots™ Optimization for a Major Textiles Company

The formula to compute the EOQ for a purchased item is as follows:

$$EOQ = \{(2 \times FAD \times POC) / (UIV \times ICR)\}^{1/2}$$

For example, if an item has an annual demand of 3,000 units per year; a purchase order cost of $300 per purchase order; a purchase price of $2,100 per unit; and an inventory carrying rate of 30% per year then its EOQ is

$$EOQ = [(2 \times 3,000 \times \$300)/(\$2,100 \times 30\%)]^{1/2} =$$
$$[(1,800,000)/(630)]^{1/2} = [2,857]^{1/2} = 53 \text{ units}$$

The formula to compute the EOQ for a manufactured item, sometimes referred to as the economic run quantity (ERQ) is as follows:

$$ERQ = \{(2 \times FAD \times SUC) / (UIV \times ICR)\}^{1/2}$$

For example, if an item has an annual demand of 5,000 units per year; a setup cost of $3,200 per setup; a standard cost of $85.00 per unit; and an inventory carrying rate of 25% per year then its EOQ is

EOQ = [(2 x 5,000 x $3,200)/($85 x 25%)] $^{\frac{1}{2}}$ = [(32,00,000)/(21.25)]$^{\frac{1}{2}}$ =
[1,505,882]$^{1/2}$ = 1,227 units

EOQ is considered passé, outdated, and nearly pre-historic in many inventory circles. Yet, in our work with the most advanced supply chain organizations around the world we are finding great profit, service, and operational improvements with EOQ.

Unit Fill Rate

The *unit fill rate* (UFR) for an item is the portion of the total number of units requested with inventory available to fill the request. It is distinct from and higher than *line fill rate* (% of lines shipped complete) and *order fill rate* (% of orders shipped complete). The target unit fill rate is a decision, not an outcome. It is perhaps the most important inventory planning decision of all.

As discussed previously, the higher the unit fill rate, the lower the lost sales cost. However, the higher the unit fill rate, the greater the inventory required to provide it, and the greater the resulting inventory carrying cost. There are many ways to determine optimal target unit fill rates. One method is to choose the unit fill rate that minimizes expected inventory policy cost. Another method is to choose the unit fill rate that maximizes expected GMROI. Still another method is to choose the unit fill rate that maximizes IVA. What do we do? It depends on the financial, service, and operational goals. The ability to visualize and simulate those relationships as demonstrated in the series of Figures 2.18 to 2.20 from the RightStock™ Inventory Optimization System is the key and often missing piece in the inventory strategy puzzle.

Safety Stock Inventory

The literal definition of *safety stock inventory* (SSI) is the inventory on-hand when a replenishment arrives (Point 7 in Figure 2.21). The average safety stock is the average on-hand inventory at the end of several replenishment cycles. Safety stock is required to support promised levels of inventory availability when the demand during a leadtime or the length of a leadtime is variable. For example, if a replenishment is delayed or if the demand during a leadtime is much greater than normal, safety stock is in place to fulfill demand until the replenishment arrives or to satisfy some portion of the excess demand. There would be no need for safety stock if we knew exactly what customers wanted, when they wanted it, and exactly when replenishments arrive. To the extent there is uncertainty in any of those three variables, safety stock is required to provide anything better than 50% inventory availability.

Reorder Point

The *reorder point* (ROP) is the inventory level at which a replenishment order is placed (Point 8 in Figure 2.21). As a rule, the reorder point is set at the leadtime demand plus safety stock.

$$ROP = LD + SSI$$

There are a variety of other inventory control policies and variables including the use of **order-up-to-levels** (OUL), the level of inventory a replenishment quantity should yield when it is placed; **review time periods** (RTP), the fixed time between inventory reviews; and a wide mix of programs for joint item replenishment.

2.9 Inventory Interdependencies

So far we have discussed the elements of inventory decision making to a large degree in isolation. The complex truth of inventory decision making is that many of the elements are inter-related. Those inter-relationships create the conflict, difficulty, and challenges of inventory decision making.

A few years ago one of our clients in the health and beauty industry asked us to help them work through those difficulties with their executives. In response we developed an inventory simulation tool that our clients now use in real-time to work through a wide range of inventory decisions. That tool, our RightStock™ Inventory Simulation System is presented in Figure

2.24. It ties together item characteristics, planning parameters, financial terms, and decision variables into a single, dynamic, visual simulation of inventory decision making. Specifically it computes key financial metrics (IVA, IPC, ICC, GM, LSC, LS, AIV, GMROI, Turns) and inventory investments (SSIV, LSIV, PIV) as a function of key planning parameters (ICR, SF, POC), item characteristics (USP, UIV, L, FAD, LFEP), and target fill rate.

A baseline scenario is presented in Figure 2.24. The baseline is from a large toy company. It presents the company's SUPER SKU; a term we use to designate a client's fictitious median SKU we sometimes use for modeling purposes. We will use the model in Chapter 3 to teach a variety of inventory decision making dynamics including RightCast™ (forecast optimization), RightTimes™ (leadtime optimization), RightLots™ (lot size optimization), RightRate™ (inventory carrying rate optimization), and RightStock™ (total inventory optimization).

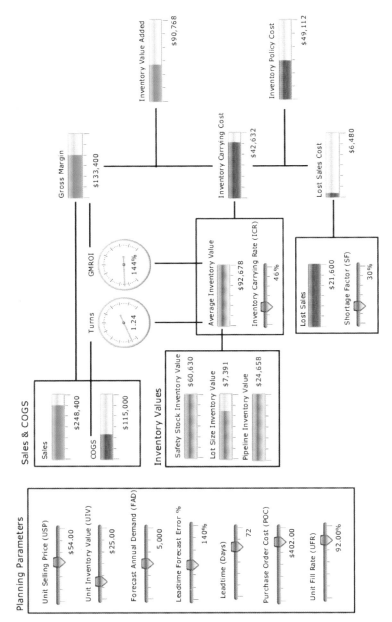

Figure 2.24 RightStock™ Inventory Simulation for a Large Toy Company

Chapter 3

Inventory Optimization

3.1 SKU Optimization

3.2 Forecast Optimization

3.3 Leadtime Optimization

3.4 Lot Size Optimization

3.5 Deployment Optimization

3.6 Visibility Optimization

3.7 Inventory Carrying Rate Optimization

I developed the RightStock™ (Figure 3.1) inventory strategy model as a part of our RightChain™ framework to help professionals work through the complexities, intricacies, and tradeoffs of inventory decision making. The model is based on 30+ years of consulting, research, and development in inventory and supply chain strategy.

RightStock™ is quantitative, logical, and methodical. It is not a philosophy unless you call not having a philosophy a philosophy, or unless you call objectively putting numbers to decisions a philosophy. The model is unique in that it works from the SKU level up. We begin by determining optimal SKU-level inventory strategies. We aggregate those into category, business unit and/or geographical strategies.

I have enjoyed teaching the RightStock™ model to hundreds of organizations and thousands of professionals from all over the world. RightStock™ is influencing the inventory strategies of some of the world's most successful supply chains including Abbott Labs, Coca-Cola, Disney, Hallmark, Honda, Nutrisystem, Pratt & Whitney, and Procter & Gamble, to name a few. So far the model is responsible for more than $1 Billion in profit improvements.

RightStock™ is a seven step journey designed to optimize (not minimize) inventory levels. The optimal inventory level is the level that meets the required service level and yields the best result for the selected financial performance metric. After establishing those financial and service performance metrics, the journey begins. The first step in the journey is *SKU optimization* (RightSKUs™), the search for the portfolio that balances financial performance with customer needs for service and variety. The second step is *forecast optimization* (RightCast™), establishing forecast accuracies that improve decision making across the entire supply chain. Next is *leadtime optimization* (RightTimes™), the computation and implementation of leadtimes that balance purchase prices, transportation costs, and inventory levels. Step four is *lot size optimization* (RightLots™), establishing lot sizes across the supply chain that balance inventory carrying costs with manufacturing setup and procurement purchase order costs. The fifth step is *deployment optimization* (RightPloy™), defining the inventory allocation to facilities that optimizes inventory carrying costs, re-deployment costs, and response times to customers. The sixth step is *visibility optimization* (RightSight™), defining and implementing the level and form of inventory visibility that yields the highest return on investment. The final step is *inventory carrying rate optimization* (RightRate™), measuring and then optimizing the opportunity cost of capital, storage and handling, loss and damage, obsolescence and mark-downs, and insurance and taxes.

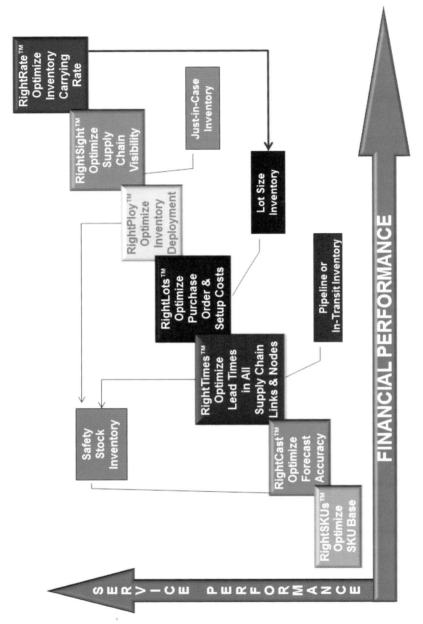

Figure 3.1 RightStock™ Inventory Model

3.1 RightSKUs™: SKU Optimization

SKU optimization, often referred to as SKU rationalization or SKU portfolio management, is one of the first, best, and most important steps in inventory strategy development. When we begin RightStock™ projects we habitually find that about a third of the SKUs are profitable, about a third are breaking even, and about a third are losing money. If you could only take one of the steps recommended in this book, this would be it.

Below are several examples of Pareto's Law working in SKU revenue and profitability. Figure 3.2 is from a RightSKUs™ analysis in a biotechnology company. 5% of the SKUs yield the first 67% of revenue; 10% yield 81%; and 20% yield 92%.

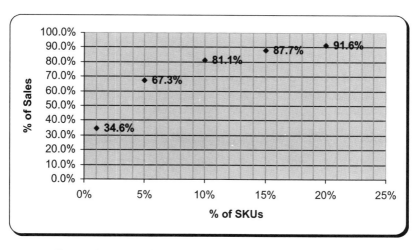

Figure 3.2 Pareto's Law at Work in Biotech SKU Revenue

Another example is in Figure 3.3. The example is from a large service parts organization. Note that 427 (8.8%) of their SKUs yield 99% of their revenue. Lamentably, 34.7% of their inventory investment, $8,732,685, was in the SKUs that yielded the last 1% of their revenue. Worse yet, over $18 million worth of new product was on order for those same bottom dwelling SKUs.

	% of Revenue	No. of SKUs	% of SKUs	On Hand $s	% On Hand $s	On Order $s	% On Order $s
A	50%	38	0.8%	$ 4,039,410	16.0%	$49,172,393	52.5%
B	80%	143	3.0%	$ 4,062,673	16.1%	$12,720,699	13.6%
C	90%	153	3.2%	$ 2,866,522	11.4%	$ 5,676,796	6.1%
D	95%	165	3.4%	$ 2,531,909	10.1%	$ 4,370,671	4.7%
E	99%	427	8.8%	$ 2,942,393	11.7%	$ 2,929,997	3.1%
F	Remainder	3,901	80.8%	$ 8,732,685	34.7%	$18,755,643	20.0%

Figure3.3 RightSKUs™ Analysis for a Large Service Parts Organization

You SKUs; you lose!

Another example of the phenomenon is illustrated in Figure 3.4. The figure is a deliverable from a recent client engagement focused on SKU strategy in the food and beverage industry. Note that 28% of the SKUs yielded the first 90% of total operating profit. 39% of the SKUs yielded the first 95% of operating profit. 28% of the SKUs yield return on invested capital lower than the corporate threshold of 10%.

Operating Profit	SKUs	% SKUs	Cum SKUs	Cum% SKUs	Inventory $s	Cum Inv$s	Total Supply Chain Cost
Negative	49	12.66%	49	12.66%	$ 1,565,462	$ 1,565,462	$ 29,540,720
0% to 5%	22	5.68%	71	18.35%	$ 1,457,217	$ 3,022,678	$ 33,483,000
6% to %10	15	3.88%	86	22.22%	$ 1,317,098	$ 4,339,776	$ 38,401,000
11% to 15%	32	8.27%	118	30.49%	$ 2,524,189	$ 6,863,965	$ 42,000,000
16% to 20%	43	11.11%	161	41.60%	$ 2,793,378	$ 9,657,343	$ 21,339,333
21% to 30%	95	24.55%	256	66.15%	$ 12,272,727	$ 21,930,070	$ 34,888,211

IVA	SKUs	% SKUs	Cum SKUs	Cum% SKUs	Inventory $s	Cum Inv$s	Total Supply Chain Cost
Negative	26	6.72%	26	6.72%	$ 270,497	$ 270,497	$ 27,991,299
$0 to $1,000	25	6.46%	51	13.18%	$ 224,322	$ 494,818	$ 31,099,543
$1,000 to $5,000	30	7.75%	81	20.93%	$ 374,084	$ 868,902	$ 33,099,798
$5,000 to $10,000	24	6.20%	105	27.13%	$ 366,336	$ 1,235,238	$ 41,222,908
$10,000 to $25,000	47	12.14%	152	39.28%	$ 1,680,720	$ 2,915,958	$ 52,772,939

GMROI	SKUs	% SKUs	Cum SKUs	Cum% SKUs	Inventory $s	Cum Inv$s	Total Supply Chain Cost
Negative	5	1.29%	5	1.29%	$ 82,853	$ 82,853	$ 27,991,299
0's	45	11.63%	50	12.92%	$ 2,420,399	$ 2,503,252	$ 31,099,543
1's	14	3.62%	64	16.54%	$ 1,839,287	$ 4,342,538	$ 33,099,798
2's	26	6.72%	90	23.26%	$ 2,890,469	$ 7,233,007	$ 41,222,908
3's	9	2.33%	99	25.58%	$ 602,301	$ 7,835,308	$ 52,772,939
4's	11	2.84%	110	28.42%	$ 411,224	$ 8,246,531	$ 28,882,221
5's	19	4.91%	129	33.33%	$ 1,517,483	$ 9,764,014	$ 17,333,119

ROIC	SKUs	% SKUs	Cum SKUs	Cum% SKUs	Inventory $s	Cum Inv$s	Total Supply Chain Cost
Negative	49	12.7%	49	12.7%	$ 1,565,462	$ 1,565,462	$ 29,540,720
0% to 5%	42	10.9%	91	23.5%	$ 3,027,972	$ 4,593,434	$ 25,342,000
6% to 10%	30	7.8%	121	31.3%	$ 4,404,671	$ 8,998,105	$ 60,285,000

Figure 3.4 RightSKUs™ Analysis in the Food & Beverage Industry

RightChain™

Their hope, as it is with many organizations, was that more SKUs would translate to more sales and profit. In Figure 3.5 you can see that the introduction of new SKUs did not yield more sales, but spread the same sales over more SKUs. Maintaining sales may seem like a victory; however the introduction of the additional SKUs and their related complexity works against supply chain, inventory, and profit performance. In this case, inventory investment grew from $51 million to $69 million; a 35% increase in inventory investment coming with a 44% increase in SKUs (Figure 3.6). To make matters worse, by spreading the same demand over more SKUs, forecast accuracy declined, resulting in significantly higher out of stock levels; growing from a low of 2% to a high of 7%; a 250% increase in out of stock rates (Figure 3.7)!

The additional warehousing space, warehouse congestion, longer pick lines, increased planning cycles, and shorter run lengths all resulted in a 27% increase in total supply chain cost per case from a low of $2.56 to a high of $3.26 (Figure 3.8). In this case turning back the clock to the good ole days of $2.56 per case was worth in excess of $50 million per year in supply chain cost savings. Lastly, without an increase in sales, with higher inventory levels, and reduced gross margins due to higher supply chain costs, GMROI declined from a high of 1143% to a low of 848%; a 26% decrease (Figure 3.9). I coined the phrase, "You SKUs, you lose." to help them remember the performance burden of more, underperforming SKUs.

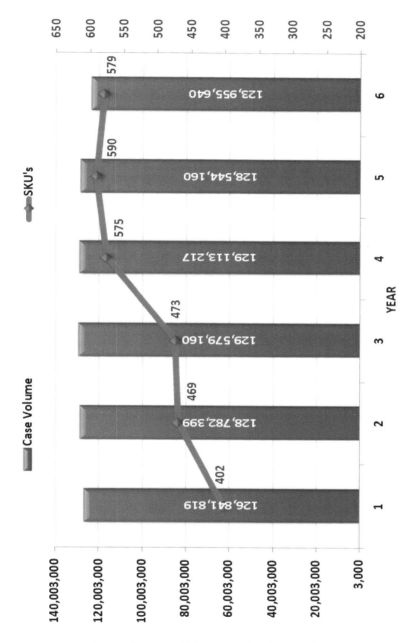

Figure 3.5 Case Volume vs. Number of SKUs

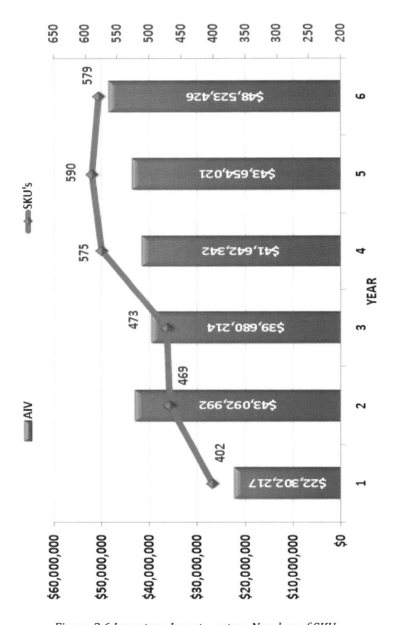

Figure 3.6 Inventory Investment vs. Number of SKUs

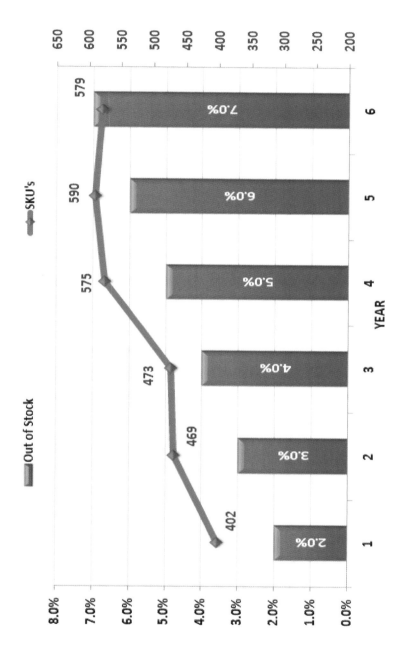

Figure 3.7 Out of Stocks vs. Number of SKUs

🐟**RightChain™**

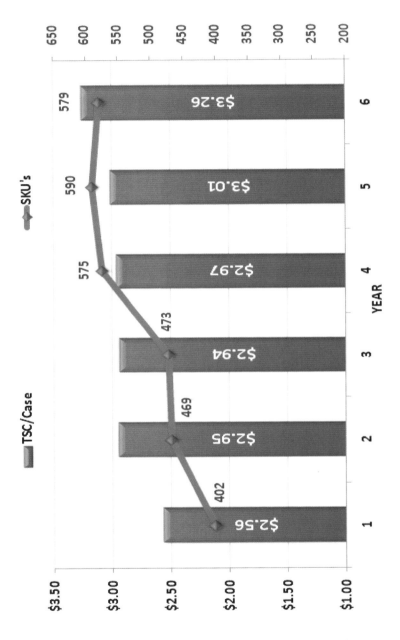

Figure 3.8 Total Supply Chain Cost per Case vs. Number of SKUs

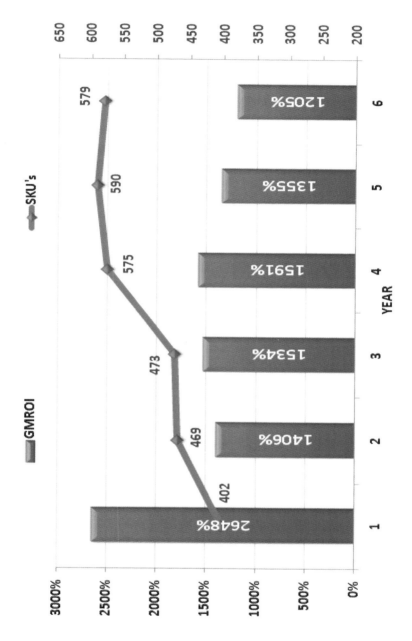

Figure 3.9 GMROI vs. Number of SKUs

But it's just a SKU.

The impact of a single SKU working in a supply chain is greatly underestimated. In this client example we established that each "little" SKU was....

- **Ordered 1,934,000 times per year....**
  - There were 1,212,000,000 SKU-Orders in a year costing $30,000,000 or $.04 per SKU-Order. Removing one SKU would potentially save $60,000.
- **Delivered 1,815,358 times per year...**
  - There were 907,679,000 SKU-Deliveries in a year costing $91,000,000 or $.10 per SKU-Delivery. Removing one SKU would potentially save $182,000.
- **Merchandised 1,063,463 times per year....**
  - There were 500,908,801 SKU-Pulls in a year costing $55,246,000, or $.09 per SKU-Pull. Removing one SKU would potentially save $110,000.
- **Picked in warehouses 120,000 times per year....**
  - There were 12,000,000 SKU-Picks in a year costing $65,000,000 or $5.42 per SKU-pick. Removing one SKU would potentially save $130,000.
- **Made or bought 60,000 times per year...**
  - There were 6,000,000 SKU-Lots in a year, costing $47,000,000 per year.
- **HANDLED IN SOME WAY 7,000,000 times per year.**

o   REMOVING ONE SKU COULD POTENTIALLY SAVE UP TO
$480,000/year;   TEN   SKUs $4,800,000/year;   ONE
HUNDRED SKUs $48,000,000/year

Pruning for Profit

In my experience the most fruitful first step to take in developing an inventory strategy is to *remove non-value added SKUs; SKUs that are more trouble than they are worth*. With those SKUs removed, the same or less inventory is much more profitably allocated to the remaining SKUs. Forecasting becomes more accurate because the same forecasting resources are focused on fewer, more forecastable SKUs. Fill rate and market share increase as a result.

The forecast accuracy for a SKU you don't have is perfect. The leadtime for a SKU you don't have is 0. The inventory investment in a SKU you don't have is $0. The cube occupied by an SKU you don't have is 0. The length of the pick line for a SKU you don't have is 0. The planning time required for a SKU you don't have is 0.

According to Webster, pruning means "to reduce especially by eliminating superfluous matter, to remove as superfluous, to cut off or cut back parts of for better shape or more fruitful growth, to cut away what is unwanted or superfluous." Pruning focuses available resources on the healthiest limbs and branches in order to maximize the quantity and the quality of the fruit.

RightChain™

One of the best examples of the profitability of pruning comes from an unexpected source... We have a franchise of our business in Japan through a joint venture with a division of Mitsubishi. I travel there once or twice a year to teach a series of seminars, consult with clients, and check up on the business. During one of my first trips, my Japanese partner promised to take me to one of the best places to eat in Tokyo – the basement of a department store near our Tokyo office. I didn't understand until I got to the produce section. He showed me some of the most beautiful fruit and vegetables I have ever seen. They were also the most expensive I have ever seen. A small bunch of grapes was $14.00. One cantaloupe was $120.00. A single strawberry was $5.00. Three peaches were $9.00. I asked my partner why the fruit was so expensive. He explained that when the fruit is newly budding on a plant, the farmers identify the most promising 10% and prune the other 90%. The full resources of the plant are then focused on the best 10% of the fruit.

The fruit was so expensive that I didn't buy any. I could only imagine what it tasted like until a client invited us into his home for dessert. My wife and two children were with me. We sat on the floor in his dining room and he proceeded to serve what I estimate was $1,000 worth of fresh fruit. It was the best fruit I have ever eaten, so good that it was as if I had never eaten fruit before.

This is obviously an extreme example of the power of pruning; but the point is the same; when it comes to SKUs, less is usually more.

One of our major food industry clients recently brought to our attention that in the short time we had been working with them the most effective initiative we had put in place was RightSKUs™. That initiative had reduced their total SKU base from 3,000 to 2,000 (a 33% reduction) and over that time their gross margin return on inventory, fill rate, and market share had increased substantially. The overall EBIT increase was in the multi-millions.

Many organizations have initiated SKU rationalization projects. Many of those projects have died on the vine. The only means we have found to successfully carry out a pruning project is to follow a facilitated methodology and to *make the project a process*. We have developed a formal methodology for SKU rationalization called RightSKUs™. Through the RightSKUs™ methodology we develop formal criteria for evaluating the value of a SKU. The project team assigns weights to each SKU valuation criteria and all SKUs are given a valuation ranking. That ranking is used and updated in an on-going process and series of RightChain™ meetings (Figure 4.15) that institutionalize the pruning process.

An example of a recent SKU valuation for a major plastics company is presented in Figure 3.10. In this particular analysis we included pounds sold, EBIT, EBIT per pound, and EBIT % in

☜RightChain™

the most valuable SKU rankings. We sometimes call the valuation a Most Valuable SKUs ranking. The ABCD categories are used in the customer service policy with service levels differentiated for A, B, and C SKUs. D SKUs are pruned.

SKU	EBIT ($000s)	EBIT Rank	Pounds (000s)	Pound Rank	EBIT/Pound	EBIT/Pound Rank	EBIT %	EBIT% Rank	Rank Sum	Value Rank	MVSKU	ABCD
3097001	$ 4,440	1.0	13,147	1	$ 0.34	9	20.9%	9	20	40	1	A
3022012	$ 2,361	2.0	7,162	3	$ 0.33	12	21.0%	8	25	39	2	A
3022022	$ 896	6.0	2,656	12	$ 0.34	10	21.1%	5	33	38	3	A
3092001	$ 1,184	4.0	4,391	5	$ 0.27	16	18.7%	13	38	37	4	A
3092002	$ 943	5.0	2,770	11	$ 0.34	8	17.7%	17	41	35	5	A
3092003	$ 531	11.0	586	28	$ 0.91	1	38.6%	1	41	35	5	A
3022031	$ 694	9.0	2,092	13	$ 0.33	11	20.0%	11	44	34	7	A
3022068	$ 850	7.0	3,683	7	$ 0.23	21	19.2%	12	47	33	8	A
3022195	$ 359	14.0	959	22	$ 0.37	5	20.2%	10	51	32	9	A
3022240	$ 1,722	3.0	10,938	2	$ 0.16	24	9.8%	26	55	29	10	A
3092007	$ 845	8.0	3,558	8	$ 0.24	20	14.7%	19	55	29	10	A
3032111	$ 252	18.0	409	33	$ 0.61	2	32.3%	2	55	29	10	A
3032259	$ 277	16.0	882	23	$ 0.31	14	21.1%	6	59	28	13	B
3061001	$ 649	10.0	3,968	6	$ 0.16	23	11.8%	23	62	27	14	B
3061006	$ 294	15.0	966	21	$ 0.30	15	18.0%	16	67	26	15	B
3061010	$ 474	12.0	3,071	10	$ 0.15	25	12.8%	22	69	24	16	B
3061012	$ 107	27.0	233	36	$ 0.46	3	24.8%	3	69	24	16	B
3061014	$ 195	19.0	620	27	$ 0.31	13	18.4%	15	74	23	18	B
3061016	$ 80	29.0	220	37	$ 0.36	6	21.5%	4	76	22	19	B
3061023	$ 412	13.0	4,475	4	$ 0.09	32	5.8%	30	79	21	20	B
3061006	$ 70	32.0	176	38	$ 0.40	4	21.0%	7	81	20	21	C
3061011	$ 101	28.0	295	35	$ 0.34	7	18.5%	14	84	19	22	C
3061012	$ 183	20.0	1,220	19	$ 0.15	26	11.5%	24	89	17	23	C
3061014	$ 124	25.0	483	29	$ 0.26	17	16.5%	18	89	17	23	C
3061016	$ 261	17.0	3,105	9	$ 0.08	33	5.5%	32	91	16	25	C
3061026	$ 130	23.0	701	26	$ 0.19	22	9.9%	25	96	15	26	C
3061031	$ 165	21.0	1,735	14	$ 0.10	31	5.7%	31	97	14	27	C
3061034	$ 139	22.0	1,229	18	$ 0.11	29	6.8%	29	98	12	28	C
3061051	$ 108	26.0	431	32	$ 0.25	19	13.8%	21	98	12	28	C
3061052	$ 129	24.0	1,117	20	$ 0.12	28	7.7%	28	100	11	30	C
3061055	$ 78	30.0	1,327	15	$ 0.06	34	4.2%	34	113	10	31	D
3051031	$ 9	36.0	37	40	$ 0.26	18	14.6%	20	114	9	32	D
3094005	$ 73	31.0	726	25	$ 0.10	30	5.4%	33	119	7	33	D
3051040	$ 55	33.0	1,303	16	$ 0.04	35	3.3%	35	119	7	33	D
3061008	$ 11	35.0	83	39	$ 0.13	27	8.4%	27	128	6	35	D
3061010	$ (23)	39.0	1,254	17	$ (0.02)	39	-1.5%	39	134	5	36	D
3061012	$ 9	37.0	753	24	$ 0.01	37	0.8%	37	135	4	37	D
3061014	$ 12	34.0	473	31	$ 0.03	36	1.3%	36	137	3	38	D
3061016	$ (3)	38.0	385	34	$ (0.01)	38	-0.5%	38	148	2	39	D
3061031	$ (170)	40.0	475	30	$ (0.36)	40	-31.5%	40	150	1	40	D

Figure 3.10 Most Valuable SKU Analysis for a Plastics Company

⊛RightChain™

Step by Step

Pruning is painful. You probably know from your personal life when you've had to cut out certain activities or certain relationships that are not profitable or are even harmful. It comes up in supply chain strategy when someone in marketing and/or product development has to face the fact that their SKU is no longer valuable. Simplification is rarely easy, or popular. It challenges the status quo. It is in vogue in many organizations to boast about the complexity of their work, even if the complexity is non-value added and self-inflicted. In contrast, simplification is profitable and one of the key common denominators of successful supply chain organizations.

Instead of radical SKU reductions, some of our clients have had success piloting and implementing SKU optimization incrementally. An example incremental SKU optimization from the CPG industry is provided in Figure 3.11. The program yielded a $7 million increase in profitability.

Once the ideal portfolio has been developed, diligence is required to maintain it. With one retail client we implemented a simple rule requiring every new SKU introduction to be accompanied by the SKU that would be pruned as a result.

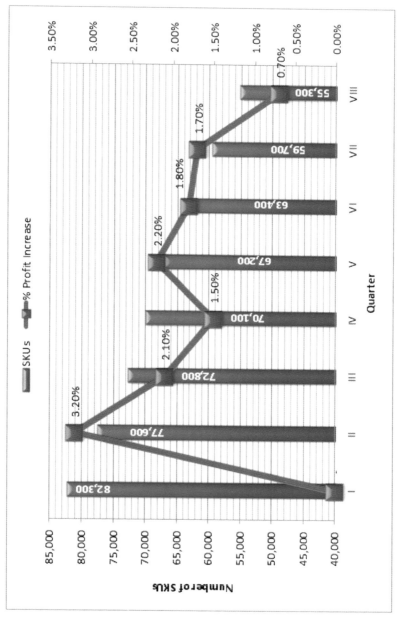

Figure 3.11 Incremental RightSKUs™ Implementation

3.2 RightCast™: Forecast Optimization

A few years ago we assisted a major sporting goods company with their inventory strategy. Based on my observations of their inventory and supply chain I made a strong recommendation to them to implement forecasting. The CIO interrupted my presentation and strongly disagreed. He said, "We are not going to do forecasting!" I was taken aback by the interruption and forcefulness of his rebuke. I asked him, "Why are you not going to forecast?" He said, "Because the forecast will be wrong." I wanted to say "Duhhhh." But I restrained myself and said. "You are right. There is only One Source of perfect forecasting Who I know, but He does not work for most supply chains. However, wouldn't you like to know how far off your forecast is, in what direction, and if it is getting better or worse?"

The CIO's strong reaction to my recommendation that they implement forecasting may sound unusual. I don't find it that far from the norm. The vast majority of organizations either don't forecast at all, forecast at such a high level that it is practically irrelevant for inventory planning purposes, and/or don't hold anybody accountable for it; which is tantamount to not forecasting at all.

Forecasting plays a pivotal and vital role in determining required inventory levels. Forecasting also influences nearly every supply chain decision. As a result, the degree to which forecasting is in error foreshadows the error in all supply chain decision making.

Even a small improvement in forecast accuracy can yield substantial inventory savings. In a recent project with a major engine manufacturer we found that every 10% improvement in forecast accuracy yielded a 5% reduction in inventory (Figure 3.12). In that particular case the reduction was worth more than $5 million in safety stock inventory.

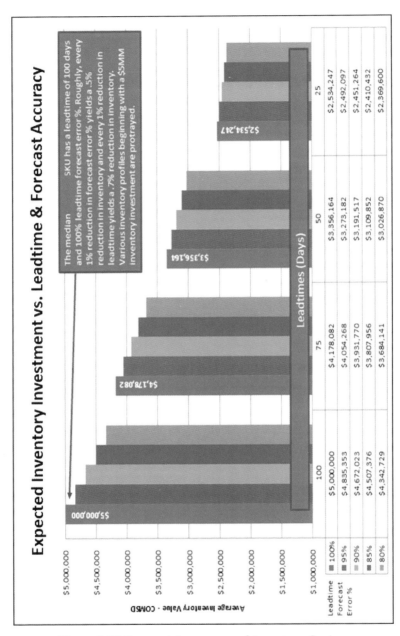

Figure 3.12 Forecast Accuracy and Inventory Savings

RightCast™ Simulation

A simulation of the benefits of forecast optimization for a single SKU for a large toy company is presented here. The baseline inventory profile for the SKU was presented in Figure 2.24.

Suppose we implement a few RightCast™ practices like forecast bias identification and minimization, individual accountability and dedication to forecast accuracy, back casting, and rapid error correction. In this case those practices helped reduce forecast error from 140% to 80% (Figure 3.13). What's the ripple effect? (Figure 3.14)

As you would expect, less safety stock inventory is required to support the same target fill rate of 92%. In this case safety stock inventory value (SSIV) declines from $60,630 to $34,646; a savings of $25,984. Average inventory value (AIV) declines by that same amount. The resulting inventory carrying cost declines from $42,632 to $30,680; a savings of $11,953 per year. Inventory turn rate increases from 1.24 to 1.72; an increase of 39%. GMROI increases from 144% to 200%; a 39% increase. Inventory Value Added™ (IVA) increases from $90,768 to $102,721; a 13% increase. Inventory Policy Cost™ (IPC) declines from $49,112 to $37,160; a 24% decrease.

Is a 43% reduction in inventory investment; a 39% increase in inventory turns; an increase in GMROI from 144% to 200%; a 13% increase in inventory value added; and a 24% decrease in inventory policy cost worth the effort? Most likely. In

🐀RightChain™

fact, we have yet to conduct a project where there was not an overwhelming business case for pursuing a RightCast™ initiative.

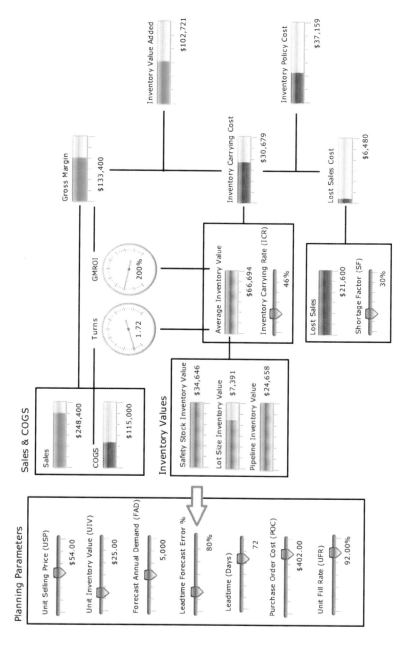

Figure 3.13 RightCast™ Simulation for a Large Toy Company

	Baseline	RightCast™	Improvement	%
Unit Selling Price (USP)	$ 54.00	$ 54.00		
- Unit Inventory Value (UIV)	$ 25.00	$ 25.00		
Unit Gross Margin (UGM)	$ 29.00	$ 29.00		
x Forecast Annual Demand (FAD)	5,000	5,000		
Gross Margin Potential (GMP)	$ 145,000.00	$145,000.00		
x Unit Fill Rate (UFR)	92.00%	92.00%		
Gross Margin (GM)	$ 133,400.00	$133,400.00		
Leadtime Forecast Error % (LFEP)	**140%**	**80%**	60%	43%
Leadtime (Days)	72	72		
Purchase Order Cost (POC)	$ 402.00	$ 402.00		
Safety Stock Inventory Value (SSIV)	**$ 60,630**	**$ 34,646**	$ 25,984	43%
+ Lot Size Inventory Value (LSIV)	$ 7,391	$ 7,391		
+ Pipeline Inventory Value (PIV)	$ 24,658	$ 24,658		
Average Inventory Value (AIV)	**$ 92,679**	**$ 66,695**	$ 25,984	28%
x Inventory Carrying Rate (ICR)	46%	46%		
Inventory Carrying Cost (ICC)	**$ 42,632**	**$ 30,680**	$ 11,953	28%
Inventory Turn Rate (ITR)	**1.24**	**1.72**	0.48	39%
GMROI	**144%**	**200%**	56%	39%
Inventory Value Added ™	**$ 90,768**	**$ 102,721**	$ 11,953	13%
Lost Sales (LS)	$ 21,600	$ 21,601		
Shortage Factor (SF)	30%	30%		
Lost Sales Cost (LSC)	$ 6,480	$ 6,480		
Inventory Policy Cost (IPC)	**$ 49,112**	**$ 37,160**	$ 11,953	24%

Figure 3.14 RightCast™ Simulation Results for a Large Toy Company

3.3 RightTimes™: Leadtime Optimization

There is a near maniacal emphasis on leadtime reduction in many organizations. A few years ago we completed a supply chain benchmarking project with a large company in the computing industry. I met a group of engineers there unlike any I have ever met; the velocity engineering group. I asked what they did. They explained that their entire purpose was to reduce cycle times in all the processes in the company. They all spoke like auctioneers and lived in their own secretive sub-culture; kind of like a secret society of cycle time ninjas. They are not the kind of people I want to hang out with, but they were very effective at taking time out of processes.

Another client recently called and asked how they could reduce their cycle time in aircraft engine repair. I asked them how long it currently takes them. They said it required seven days – including the roundtrip to Europe. Given how short the cycle time already was, I was stunned that they were even asking. They insisted I consider the question. I asked them what the cycle time was before it had been reduced to seven days. They said it had been 21 days. I asked them how they condensed the cycle time to seven days. They said they value stream mapped the process into daily buckets and found opportunities to work activities in parallel and to eliminate wasted time. I encouraged them to repeat the process, but to use hourly buckets and to look specifically at which days in the week and hours in a day each activity would be performed. They took my

☜RightChain™

suggestion and are now working the international process in 4.5 days.

Leadtime often plays a dominant role in the inventory required to support a supply chain strategy. It contributes directly to pipeline and safety stock inventory.

In safety stock inventory, leadtime has a multiplicative effect. My friend at Honda, Chuck Hamilton, uses a golf analogy to explain the effect. If a golfer hits a ball 100 yards off the tee with the face off center by 10%, the ball is only 10 yards off center at the end of its flight, and still in the fairway. If a golfer hits a ball 200 yards off the tee with the face off center by 10%, the ball is 20 yards off center at the end of its flight, and barely in the fairway. If a golfer hits a ball 300 yards off the tee with the face off center by 10%, the ball is off center by 30 yards at the end of its flight, in the rough, probably the deep rough. The longer the leadtime, the greater the impact of forecast errors.

In a recent project with a large food company we found that every day of leadtime reduction was worth approximately $5 million (Figure 3.15).

Given these results, the logical assumption is that shorter leadtimes are better. At the risk of being heretical, I would say that *the right leadtime is better*. Many customers do not value speed but prefer leadtime consistency. Many customers, suppliers, and internal systems are not equipped to accommodate reduced leadtimes. Also, leadtime reductions have a price tag. Some leadtimes are shortened by moving product more frequently by more expensive transportation modes (e.g. air vs. ocean, truck vs. rail, etc.). Some leadtimes are reduced by purchasing from local suppliers at a higher price. Some leadtimes are reduced via forward stocking nearer the point of consumption, requiring extra inventory. Some leadtimes are reduced by investing in material handling automation to speed product through warehouses, distribution centers, ports, and factories. Those investments must be weighed against the benefits associated with the leadtime reductions they bring.

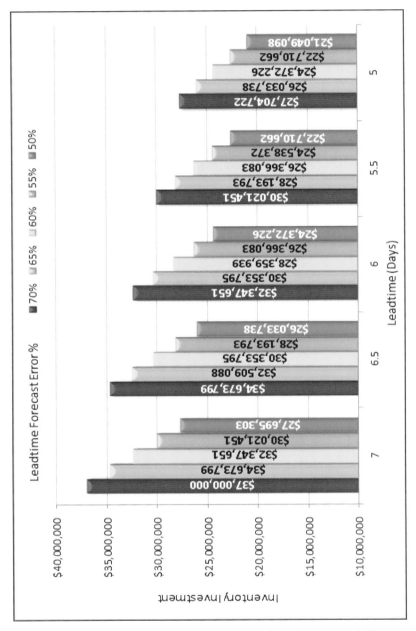

Figure 3.15 Inventory Investment vs. Days of Leadime – Food Client

RightTimes™ Simulation

Determining the appropriate investment in leadtime reduction is the purpose of RightTimes™ optimization and simulation. An example RightTimes™ simulation for a single SKU for a large toy company is presented in Figure 3.16. In the example a variety of leadtime reduction options were under consideration including alternate transportation modes, alternate transportation schedules, near-sourcing, and receiving automation. Those options had the potential to reduce leadtime from the baseline of 72 days to 40 days. What is the ripple effect? (Figure 3.17) How much could be justifiably invested in the options?

First, notice that safety stock inventory value drops from $60,330 to $33,683; a reduction of $26,947 or 44%. Pipeline inventory investment drops from $24,650 to $13,699; a reduction of $10,951 or 44%. Total inventory investment drops from $92,679 to $54,773; a reduction of $37,906 or 41%. Inventory carrying cost drops from $42,632 to $25,196; a reduction of $17,437 per year. Inventory turns increase from 1.24 to 2.10; a 69% increase. GMROI increases from 144% to 244%. Inventory value added increases from $90,768 to $108,204; a $17,437 increase or 19%. Inventory policy cost drops from $49,112 to $31,676; a reduction of $17,437 or 36%.

Is a 41% reduction in inventory investment; a 69% increase in inventory turns; a 100% increase in GMROI; a 19% increase in inventory value added; and a 36% reduction in

◈RightChain™

inventory policy cost worth the investment? In this case those percentages applied to the entire SKU base, yielded a $20,000,000 reduction in inventory; $8 million per year reduction in inventory carrying costs; turns increasing from 1.2 to 2.0; an increase in GMROI from 150% to 250%; and an increase in inventory value added of over $17 million. The investments in alternate transportation modes and routes, near-sourcing, and automated logistics and material handling systems required to accomplish the leadtime reduction totaled approximately $4.5 million; yielding a payback against inventory carrying cost savings of 0.56 years.

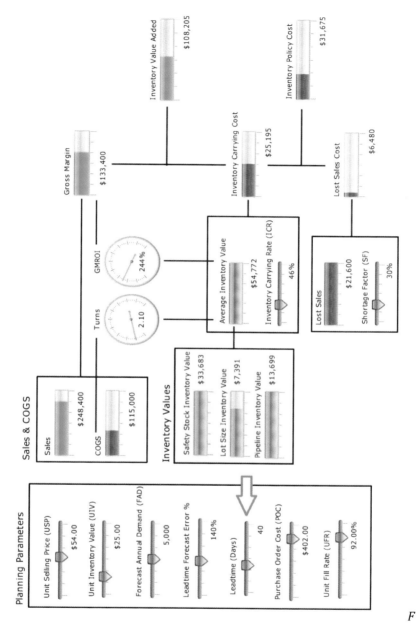

igure 3.16 RightTimes™ Leadtime Simulation for a Large Toy Company

F

RightChain™

Factor	Baseline	RightTimes™	Improvement	%
Unit Selling Price (USP)	$ 54.00	$ 54.00		
- Unit Inventory Value (UIV)	$ 25.00	$ 25.00		
Unit Gross Margin (UGM)	$ 29.00	$ 29.00		
x Forecast Annual Demand (FAD)	5,000	5,000		
Gross Margin Potential (GMP)	$ 145,000.00	$145,000.00		
x Unit Fill Rate (UFR)	92.00%	92.00%		
Gross Margin (GM)	$ 133,400.00	$133,400.00		
Leadtime Forecast Error % (LFEP)	140%	140%		
Leadtime (Days)	72	40	32	44%
Purchase Order Cost (POC)	$ 402.00	$ 402.00		
Safety Stock Inventory Value (SSIV)	$ 60,630	$ 33,683	$ 26,947	44%
+ Lot Size Inventory Value (LSIV)	$ 7,391	$ 7,391		
+ Pipeline Inventory Value (PIV)	$ 24,658	$ 13,699		
Average Inventory Value (AIV)	$ 92,679	$ 54,773	$ 37,906	41%
x Inventory Carrying Rate (ICR)	46%	46%		
Inventory Carrying Cost (ICC)	$ 42,632	$ 25,196	$ 17,437	41%
Inventory Turn Rate (ITR)	1.24	2.10	0.86	69%
GMROI	144%	244%	100%	69%
Inventory Value Added ™	$ 90,768	$ 108,204	$ 17,437	19%
Lost Sales (LS)	$ 21,600	$ 21,601		
Shortage Factor (SF)	30%	30%		
Lost Sales Cost (LSC)	$ 6,480	$ 6,480		
Inventory Policy Cost (IPC)	$ 49,112	$ 31,676	$ 17,437	36%

Figure 3.17 RightTimes™ Simulation Results for a Large Toy Company

3.4 RightLots™: Lot Size Optimization

To teach lot size optimization I like to use an example that is close to home. Suppose you live in Georgia and there is only one ATM machine in the state. The single ATM is located in a small, remote town in south Georgia (Are there other kinds?). The ATM is only open during the last week of July. For whatever cash you need you endure a trip down heavily congested country roads through swarms of gnats in humidity so thick you will need an umbrella in heat so intense you will think you are in a sauna to stand in lines so long you will think you are at Disney World. One last thing. When you finally get your turn at the ATM the fee to withdraw your money is $1,000. How much money will you withdraw? Yep. All of it. While it is not in the bank, it is not earning interest. It is likely to get lost or stolen, and if you are like me you are much more likely to spend it.

The sum total of the hassle, pain, and literal withdrawal fee equate to the transaction cost. In general, the higher the transaction cost, the fewer times we want to endure the transaction.

In manufacturing and production contexts, the transaction cost related to lot sizing is the cost, hassle and time of setting up or changing over a production line. The higher the cost, the longer the time, the greater the hassle, the fewer times we want to execute the transaction. So, when we get the line setup, we should wisely run it for a while. The result may be a lot of inventory. (No wonder it's called a lot size.)

⊛RightChain™

In the purchasing and procurement context, the cost related to the time, telecommunications, planning, and execution of a purchase order is the transaction cost. As was the case with production, the higher the cost, the longer the time, and the greater the hassle, the fewer times we want to execute the transaction. So, when it comes time to place a purchase order, we are going to order a lot.

Now, let's run the south Georgia ATM tape back and fast forward to another time. Suppose there is an ATM machine within arm's reach wherever you are. It is open 7x24x365. There is no "withdrawal" fee. (Amazingly, it's free to access your own money.) Now, how much will you withdraw each time? Yes, just enough for the next few minutes or until some cash is needed.

In manufacturing, if it's free and requires no time to setup or changeover a line, we can afford as many setups as we wish. Manufacturing lot size inventory in those cases should be minimal. In procurement, if it's cost and hassle free to place a purchase order, we can afford to place as many as we like. Procurement lot size inventory in those cases should be minimal.

Transaction costs should go a long way toward determining the size of the transaction. Surprisingly, not many supply chain organizations can tell you the true cost of their most important supply chain transactions; setup costs, changeover costs, purchase order cost, freight bill payment costs, transportation setup costs, etc.. As a result, lot sizing is often overlooked as an opportunity to improve inventory and supply chain performance. Lot sizing has become a lost science in supply chain optimization. Even EOQ is one of the babies thrown out with the bath water.

In an attempt to re-institute lot sizing in supply chain strategy, we developed and execute lot size deviation analyses as a part of most supply chain assessments. We typically find that lot sizes are off in one direction or another by 100% to 300%. An example from a large food and beverage company is in Figure 3.18. Note that the lot sizes for 86.5% of the SKUs were undersized; to the tune of 50% of the optimal lot size. Once corrected, total supply chain costs were reduced by more than $10 million; the majority of those savings accruing from higher manufacturing productivity .

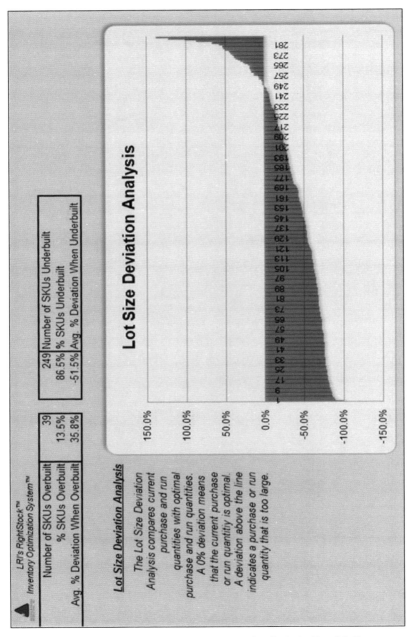

Figure 3.18. RightLots™ Lot Size Deviation Analysis in Food & Beverage

RightLots™ Simulation

Just as the prevailing trade press winds have blown toward lower and lower inventory, they have carried with them the move toward smaller and smaller lot sizes; highly flexible production cells; mixed model rapid changeovers; and lot sizes approaching one. In many cases and for many SKUs there is a high return on investment for reducing lot sizes, and in many cases there is not. Computing and implementing optimal lot sizes for manufacturing run lengths and purchasing lot sizes is the focus of RightLots™ - lot size optimization. An example lot size simulation is illustrated in Figure 3.19 and 3.20.

In the example, procurement process mapping, e-procurement, blanket ordering, and receiving automation were all under consideration. In combination those initiatives were estimated to reduce the purchase order cost from $402 per purchase order to $100 per purchase order. As you would expect, the optimal lot size inventory is significantly reduced; from $7,391 to $3,686; a 50% reduction in lot size inventory value. However, since lot size inventory represents only a small portion of total inventory in this case, the reduction in lot size inventory only yielded a 4% reduction in expected total inventory investment. The related percentage improvements to inventory carrying rate, turns, GMROI, inventory value added, and inventory policy cost are on a similar, negligible scale, ranging from 2% to 4%.

RightChain™

As a result, in this situation, work to reduce purchase order and setup cost should take a back seat to higher priority work on safety stock and pipeline inventory. That is not always the case. In many projects we engage, lot size inventory comprises the majority of total inventory value and excess inventory. In those cases lot size inventory should be the focal point for inventory optimization.

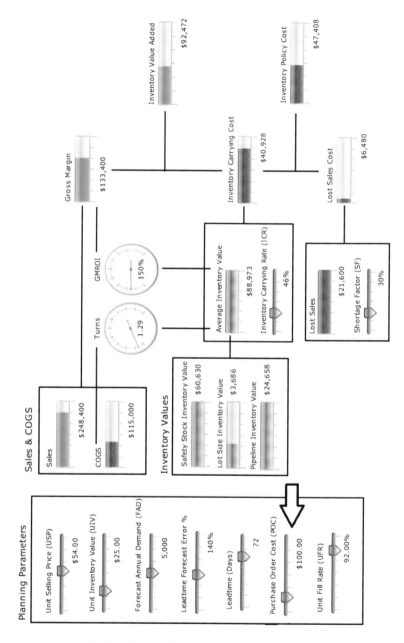

Figure 3.19 RightLots™ Simulation for a Large Toy Company

RightChain™

Factor	Baseline	RightLots™	Improvement	%
Unit Selling Price (USP)	$ 54.00	$ 54.00		
- Unit Inventory Value (UIV)	$ 25.00	$ 25.00		
Unit Gross Margin (UGM)	$ 29.00	$ 29.00		
x Forecast Annual Demand (FAD)	5,000	5,000		
Gross Margin Potential (GMP)	$ 145,000.00	$145,000.00		
x Unit Fill Rate (UFR)	92.00%	92.00%		
Gross Margin (GM)	$ 133,400.00	$133,400.00		
Leadtime Forecast Error % (LFEP)	140%	140%		
Leadtime (Days)	72	72		
Purchase Order Cost (POC)	$ 402.00	$ 100.00		
Safety Stock Inventory Value (SSIV)	$ 60,630	$ 60,630		
+ **Lot Size Inventory Value (LSIV)**	$ 7,391	$ 3,686	$ 3,705	50%
+ Pipeline Inventory Value (PIV)	$ 24,658	$ 24,658		
Average Inventory Value (AIV)	$ 92,679	$ 88,974	$ 3,705	4%
x Inventory Carrying Rate (ICR)	46%	46%		
Inventory Carrying Cost (ICC)	$ 42,632	$ 40,928	$ 1,704	4%
Inventory Turn Rate (ITR)	1.24	1.29	0.05	4%
GMROI	144%	150%	6%	4%
Inventory Value Added ™	$ 90,768	$ 92,472	$ 1,704	2%
Lost Sales (LS)	$ 21,600	$ 21,601		
Shortage Factor (SF)	30%	30%		
Lost Sales Cost (LSC)	$ 6,480	$ 6,480		
Inventory Policy Cost (IPC)	$ 49,112	$ 47,408	$ 1,704	3%

Figure 3.20 RightLots™ Simulation Results for a Large Toy Company

3.5 RightPloy™: Inventory Deployment Optimization

Sometimes it's not the amount of inventory but where it is located that makes the difference. The allocation and assignment of inventory to multiple locations is inventory deployment. It is one of the most complex inventory strategy decisions because it opens up interdependencies with customer response times, transportation costs, and re-deployment costs and concerns. I always advise our clients that all things being equal, fewer stocking locations is better than more.

What is the likelihood of a mis-deployment if there is only one facility? Zero. Once the deployment can of worms is opened, the range of options is nearly endless running from a single, central facility to consigned inventory in every customer location. Determining where to land in that spectrum is deployment optimization.

The range of deployment scenarios is nearly infinite. We recommend a rigorous process to narrow the options to a few high potential candidate deployment scenarios for evaluation. The process includes collecting and analyzing a comprehensive data base to support the decision making, brainstorming to identify candidate deployment scenarios and scenario evaluation criteria, and rigorous analytical modeling. We have been down those roads a few times. The best way to teach deployment optimization may be to share a few examples.

RightChain™

Everybody Wants a Warehouse

A few years ago we developed a supply chain strategy for the spares group in a large semi-conductor company. The catalyst for the project was a request from their sales group to provide each customer with their own spares warehouse located inside each customer's facility. That's great customer service, but very expensive. It was an easy thing for sales to request since they were not paying for inventory or supply chain expenses.

We were engaged to help the company determine conditions under which customers "earned" their own warehouse. We developed a deployment simulation system to help them answer the question on an on-going basis (Figure 3.21).

We began by working with finance to develop a return on asset threshold for customer warehouses. Based on estimated revenue, inventory consumption, and location logistics, we estimated return on assets (ROA) for on-site stocking for each customer. Customers were assigned on-site inventory based on their predicted ROA. Customers who did not qualify for the on-site spares program were given the option to increase volume to qualify.

Sales and marketing accepted the responsibility of the additional supply chain costs of supporting on-site inventories. The key was having finance, sales, and supply chain collaborating to work through the decision with reliable data and a real-time decision support tool.

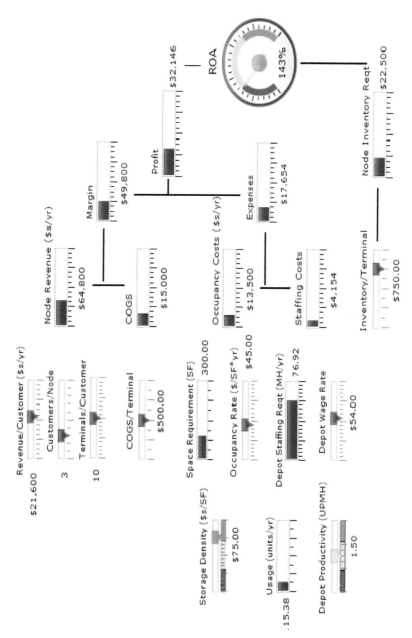

Figure 3.21 Deployment Optimization for Semi-Conductor Parts

Pre-deploy it!

One of our clients is a large food company delivering on a DSD basis to grocery chains around the southeast. Their historical deployment strategy had been to centralize and hold inventory, delaying deployment as late as required delivery windows would permit. The approach was based on the lean principle of inventory postponement; holding back inventory in a central location until an order is received. It could be called delayed deployment or deploy-to-order.

Based on their outbound transportation cost I suspected the approach might be overly expensive. They were willing to have a look at some other options. The resulting analysis is presented in Figure 3.22. The figure is a screen shot from our Multi-Echelon Inventory Optimization System. The system considers multiple network configuration options for each SKU. Network configuration options are defined as the number of central warehouses, the number of regional warehouses, and the number of local warehouses. In the example a single central warehouse serves 12 sales centers which each serve 17 small depots. Based on minimizing total logistics cost including transportation, inventory carrying, and lost sales cost, an optimal inventory deployment emerges. The key is to understand the optimal allocation and assignment of inventory for each type of SKU. In this particular case the recommended deployment is 20/30/50; 20% of the inventory held centrally; 30% held regionally; and 50% deployed in depot locations near large customers. The previous deployment had been 60/20/20. The revised deployment was worth $12 million in total logistics cost savings.

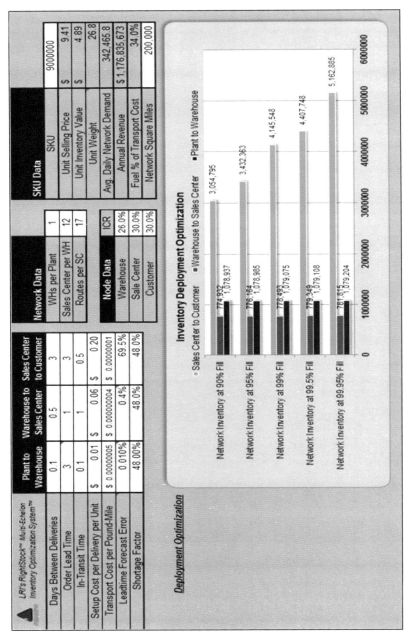

Figure 3.22 Multi-Echelon Deployment Optimization

Serving the World from Cleveland

Sometimes it goes the other way. A few years ago one of our industrial supplies clients asked us to help them with a global network strategy. The company is headquartered in Cleveland, Ohio, and served all of Europe and Asia from there. Their Asian business had grown quite rapidly and they suspected that an Asian distribution hub might be necessary and beneficial to improve customer service and reduce supply chain costs. Their intuition was logical. Certainly it would be faster and less expensive to serve Asia from Asia? Not necessarily!

As we normally do, we developed a few candidate scenarios. Since over half their Asian business was in Japan, one candidate scenario was a Japan hub. It turned out that due to poor schedules out of Japan for their cargo and excellent schedules provided by their carrier in Cleveland, it would take longer to serve their Asian clients from Japan than from Cleveland. In addition, because of the high cost of Japanese space and labor and the extra handling step required to add a hub, supply chain costs were higher.

Since Singapore was their second largest Asian market and since Singapore is an excellent logistics hub, a Singapore hub was the other option we considered. The Singapore option turned out to offer slightly better service -- a half-day closer in the worst case -- but was still more expensive, $500,000 additional per year. Is a half a day better service in the worst case worth $500,000? That's an answer the executives have to

⊛RightChain™

provide. In this case I suggested they pilot a small DC with a 3PL and monitor the result. So far, Cleveland is looking better and better.

Supply chain logistics is non-linear; often counter-intuitive. The more interdependencies there are, the more non-linear and counter-intuitive it becomes. That's why it is so important to work with comprehensive and holistic analytical models in considering each unique supply chain situation.

3.6 RightSight™: Inventory Visibility Optimization

Inventory levels to a large degree are about trust. Since we tend to not trust what we can't see, any blind spots or poor visibility in the supply chain will be places where excess inventory accumulates. The value of visibility is *replacing information about inventory for inventory*.

During a project with a home improvement company I sat with one of their buyers for an hour to get familiar with his work. Early in the hour he placed a large order for a replenishment of lumber. Toward the end of the hour he placed the same order for the same quantity with the same vendor. I asked why. He explained that if he did not receive electronic notification from the vendor that they had received the order, then he re-ordered. I asked him if he cancelled the original order. He said no. I asked why he had not cancelled the original order. He said that he wanted to make double sure the vendor received the order. I asked him if he was afraid of having too much inventory. He said no, explaining that the person in his position prior to him had been fired for running out. The lack of visibility, in this case the lack of an electronic acknowledgement from the supplier, led to excess inventory.

Inventory accuracy is a major contributor to inventory visibility. Suppose you are a buyer for a retailer and you get to keep your job if the stores in your region do not run out of stock. However, the warehouse for your region has an inventory accuracy of 60%, as was the case in a recent engagement. How much extra inventory will you procure? At least 40%, but potentially more. If the accuracy is that poor, then it would be difficult to trust any number reported by that DC.

The appetite for inventory visibility in the supply chain is nearly insatiable. With bar codes, QR codes, RFID tags, and GPS; nearly any level of inventory visibility is feasible. The difficult question is what level and type of visibility is valuable? Just like other investment decisions, there are marginal returns toward the tail end of the benefits curve. The proper approach is to develop progressively more comprehensive visibility scenarios, estimate the return and investment for each, and choose a visibility path forward. We call that RightSight™, determining the most appropriate points, transactions, and types of inventory visibility in the supply chain.

Our RightSight™ scenario generation template is provided in Figure 3.23. We consider each document, each transaction, each node, and each link in the supply chain and

◈RightChain™

recommend the optimal level and type of visibility. We measure the degree of visibility as the percent of SKUs and percent of supply chain transactions in compliance with the visibility program.

		Documents							Inventory			
		PO	ASN	BOL	Forecast	BOM	Work Order	Mnt Sched	At Supplier	In Transit	In Warehouse	At Customer
Supplier	Response	Seconds	Minutes	Hours	Days	x Days	Days	Weeks	Seconds	Seconds	Seconds	Seconds
	Frequency	Daily	On Demand	Daily	Weekly	Weekly	Daily	Weekly	On Demand	On Demand	On Demand	On Demand
	Granularity	Order Line	Doc #	Doc #	Unit	Doc #	Order Line	Order Line	Order Line	Order Line	Order Line	Order Line
	Format	XML	XML	Email	Email	XML	Efax	Email	EDI	XML	EDI	EDI
Client	Response	x Seconds	Minutes	Hours	Days	x Days	Days	Weeks	Seconds	Seconds	Minutes	Hours
	Frequency	On Demand	On Demand	On Demand	On Demand	Weekly	On Demand	On Demand	On Demand	On Demand	On Demand	On Demand
	Granularity	Order Line	Order Line	Unit	Order Line	Order Line	Unit	Order Line	Order Line	Order Line	Order Line	Order Line
	Format	MMS	MMS	MMS	Efax	MMS	MMS	MMS	MMS	Fax	XML	MMS
Customer	Response	Minutes	Minutes	Hours	Days	x Days	Days	Weeks	Seconds	Seconds	Hours	Seconds
	Frequency	On Demand	On Demand	On Demand	Hourly	Hourly	On Demand	On Demand	On Demand	On Demand	On Demand	On Demand
	Granularity	Order Line	Order Line	Order Line	Order Line	Order Line	Order Line	Order Line	Order Line	Doc #	Order Line	Unit
	Format	MMS	MMS	XML	MMS	MMS	MMS	MMS	MMS	EDI	MMS	MMS
4PL	Response	Minutes	Minutes	Hours	Days	x Days	Days	Weeks	Seconds	x Hours	Seconds	Hours
	Frequency	On Demand	Hourly	On Demand	Daily	On Demand	On Demand	On Demand	On Demand	On Demand	On Demand	On Demand
	Granularity	Order Line	Doc #	Order Line	Unit	Order Line	Order Line	Order Line	Unit	Order Line	Unit	Doc #
	Format	MMS	Fax	MMS	MMS	MMS	Email	MMS	MMS	Fax	MMS	MMS

Figure 3.23 RightSight™ Visiblity Solution Template

RightChain™

3.7 RightRate™: Inventory Carrying Rate Optimization

Inventory carrying rate is the cost of carrying a dollar of inventory for one year. It includes the opportunity cost of capital, the cost of storage and handling, loss and damage, obsolescence and mark-downs, and insurance and taxes. The rate determines the financial viability of holding inventory. If it is inexpensive to carry inventory, then it becomes less expensive to provide higher fill rates and shorter response times. Inventory carrying rate is a critical factor in nearly all inventory calculations, yet very few organizations recognize it or compute it.

Since few organizations have an inventory carrying rate, very little understanding of its impact on inventory strategy has been developed. Even when companies have an inventory carrying rate, they assume it is fixed. They overlook the fact that it, like forecast accuracy, leadtime, purchase order cost, setup cost, etc. plays a major role in inventory optimization. Inventory carrying rate should be evaluated as a potential for process improvement and investment. For example, warehouse process improvements and related MHE and WMS investments typically yield higher warehouse labor productivity, higher warehouse storage density, higher levels of inventory accuracy, and lower damage and loss rates. As a result, storage and handling costs can be significantly reduced; yielding a much lower inventory carrying rate. In addition, relocating to locales with lower interest, tax, and duty rates yields lower inventory carrying rates. One of our industrial supplies clients moved their distribution operations three blocks and paid for the move and a fully automated DC with the savings they achieved in inventory carrying costs. The savings accrued from a lower inventory carrying rate. The lower rate was the result of lower inventory taxes in the adjacent county and the free trade zone status available in the new facility.

RightRate™ Simulation

An inventory strategy considering relocation and DC automation was being considered in the example in Figure 3.24. It was thought that there was the potential to reduce the inventory carrying rate from 46% to 20% per year. The expected inventory investment increases slightly, by 4%; however the cost to carry the inventory drops dramatically, by 55%: yielding a 26% increase in inventory value added and a 43% decrease in inventory policy cost. In this case, those percentages represented savings in excess of $7 million per year in inventory carrying and total supply chain costs; an increase of over $3 million per year in inventory value added and EVA to the client. Those savings easily paid for the $2.5 million investment required for warehouse process improvements and MHE/WMS investments.

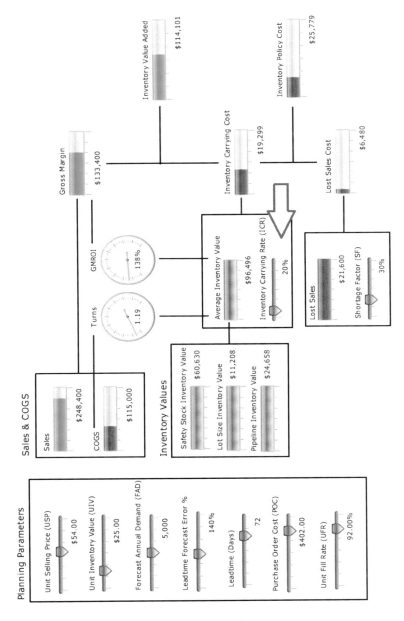

Figure 3.24 RightRate™ Simulation for a Large Toy Company

Factor	Baseline	RightRate™	Delta	%
Unit Selling Price (USP)	$ 54.00	$ 54.00		
- Unit Inventory Value (UIV)	$ 25.00	$ 25.00		
Unit Gross Margin (UGM)	$ 29.00	$ 29.00		
x Forecast Annual Demand (FAD)	5,000	5,000		
Gross Margin Potential (GMP)	$ 145,000.00	$ 145,000.00		
x Unit Fill Rate (UFR)	92.00%	92.00%		
Gross Margin (GM)	$ 133,400.00	$ 133,400.00		
Leadtime Forecast Error % (LFEP)	140%	140%		
Leadtime (Days)	72	72		
Purchase Order Cost (POC)	$ 402.00	$ 402.00		
Safety Stock Inventory Value (SSIV)	$ 60,630	$ 60,630		
+ Lot Size Inventory Value (LSIV)	$ 7,391	$ 11,208	$ (3,817)	-52%
+ Pipeline Inventory Value (PIV)	$ 24,658	$ 24,658		
Average Inventory Value (AIV)	$ 92,679	$ 96,496	$ (3,817)	-4%
x Inventory Carrying Rate (ICR)	46%	20%		
Inventory Carrying Cost (ICC)	$ 42,632	$ 19,299	$ 23,333	55%
Inventory Turn Rate (ITR)	1.24	1.19	(0.05)	-4%
GMROI	144%	138%	-6%	-4%
Inventory Value Added ™	$ 90,768	$ 114,101	$ 23,333	26%
Lost Sales (LS)	$ 21,600	$ 21,601		
Shortage Factor (SF)	30%	30%		
Lost Sales Cost (LSC)	$ 6,480	$ 6,480		
Inventory Policy Cost (IPC)	$ 49,112	$ 25,779	$ 23,333	48%

Figure 3.25 RightRate™ Simulation Results for a Large Toy Company

⊛RightChain™

3.8 RightStock™: Inventory Optimization

Because they are synergistic in their effect, a well developed inventory strategy should consider all seven RightStock™ principles – SKU assortment, forecast accuracy, leadtime, lot sizing, deployment, visibility, and inventory carrying rate - together. That was our accepted recommendation for this particular client. The results are presented in Figure 3.26 and 3.27. Forecast error was reduced from 140% to 80%. Leadtime was reduced from 72 days to 40 days. Purchase order cost was reduced from $402 to $100 per transaction. Inventory carrying rate was reduced from 46% per year to 20% per year. As a result, every type of inventory was reduced dramatically; yielding an overall reduction in total inventory investment of 58%. Inventory carrying cost for the simulated SKU was reduced from $42,632 per year to $7,707 per year; an 82% decrease. Inventory turns increased from 1.24 to 2.98; a 140% increase. GMROI increased from 144% to 346%. Inventory value added increased from $90,768 to $125,693; a 38% increase. Inventory policy cost declined from $49,112 to $14,187; a 71% decline.

Is a 58% reduction in inventory; an 82% reduction in inventory carrying cost; a 140% increase in inventory turns; an increase in GMROI from 144% to 346%; a 38% increase in inventory value added, and a 71% decrease in inventory policy cost with no decrease in an already optimized service level worth the time, effort, and investment? In this case that combination of numbers represented over $40 million worth of inventory; $10 million per year savings in inventory carrying cost; $6.5 million in inventory value added; and $10 million in inventory policy cost reductions; easily paying for the $3.5 million investment required to accomplish them.

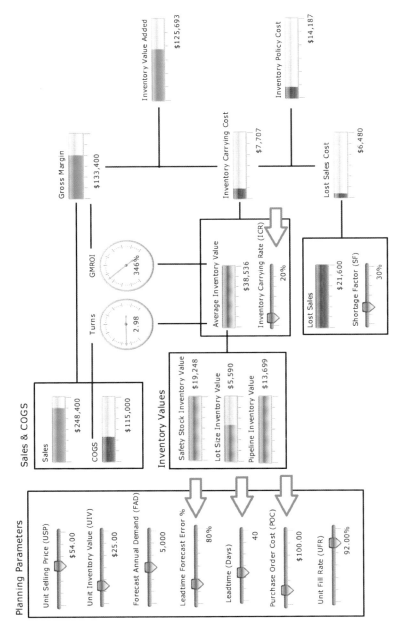

Figure 3.26 RightStock™ Simulation for a Large Toy Company

Factor	Baseline	RightStock™	Improvement	%
Unit Selling Price (USP)	$ 54.00	$ 54.00		
- Unit Inventory Value (UIV)	$ 25.00	$ 25.00		
Unit Gross Margin (UGM)	$ 29.00	$ 29.00		
x Forecast Annual Demand (FAD)	5,000	5,000		
Gross Margin Potential (GMP)	$ 145,000.00	$145,000.00		
x Unit Fill Rate (UFR)	92.00%	92.00%		
Gross Margin (GM)	$ 133,400.00	$133,400.00		
Leadtime Forecast Error % (LFEP)	140%	80%	60%	43%
Leadtime (Days)	72	40	32	44%
Purchase Order Cost (POC)	$ 402.00	$ 100.00	$ 302	75%
Safety Stock Inventory Value (SSIV)	$ 60,630	$ 19,248	$ 41,382	68%
+ Lot Size Inventory Value (LSIV)	$ 7,391	$ 5,590	$ 1,801	24%
+ Pipeline Inventory Value (PIV)	$ 24,658	$ 13,699	$ 10,959	44%
Average Inventory Value (AIV)	$ 92,679	$ 38,537	$ 54,142	58%
x Inventory Carrying Rate (ICR)	46%	20%	26%	57%
Inventory Carrying Cost (ICC)	$ 42,632	$ 7,707	$ 34,925	82%
Inventory Turn Rate (ITR)	1.24	2.98	1.74	140%
GMROI	144%	346%	202%	140%
Inventory Value Added ™	$ 90,768	$ 125,693	$ 34,925	38%
Lost Sales (LS)	$ 21,600	$ 21,601		
Shortage Factor (SF)	30%	30%		
Lost Sales Cost (LSC)	$ 6,480	$ 6,480		
Inventory Policy Cost (IPC)	$ 49,112	$ 14,187	$ 34,925	71%

Figure 3.27 RightStock™ Simulation Results for a Large Toy Company

Chapter 4

Inventory in

Supply Chain Strategy

Though often treated as such, inventory is not an end; it is a means to an end. That end is an integrated supply chain strategy supporting the business strategy. Inventory is part of that whole. Naively, it is often myopically viewed in isolation from the other elements of a supply chain.

Inventory should work synergistically with customer service, supply, transportation, and warehousing to comprise a supply chain and the logistics within it. Those interdependencies must be understood and modeled to optimize a supply chain strategy and the inventory levels required to support it. This chapter presents those interdependencies and models. We begin with the definition of "logistics", "supply chain", and "supply chain logistics".

4.1 Inventory and Logistics

There are many definitions of logistics circulating in the world of supply chain management - almost as many as there are supply chains. We developed a simple definition over 20 years ago. *Logistics is the flow of material, information and money between consumers and suppliers.*

Much can be learned from the three parts of that simple sentence. First, logistics is "flow". Flow is a good thing! What happens to water when it stops flowing? Stagnation, scum, insects, and possibly death. What happens to blood when it stops flowing? The nerds in the group always say, "coagulation". The non-nerds usually just say, "somebody dies." The point is, when material, information, and money stop flowing, some elements of the business and supply chain become unhealthy and potentially die. Even the highest performing professionals may lose their jobs when those flows stop. Customers and shareholders become disgruntled when those flows stop. Flow is a good thing!

Second, material, information, and money should flow ***simultaneously, in real-time and without paper***.

Lastly, logistics flow should be viewed, considered, and modeled bi-directionally, "between consumers and suppliers". Otherwise, its design will be sub-optimal.

We can also learn about "logistics" from its root, "logic". According to Webster, "logic" means "reason or sound judgment". Unfortunately reason and sound judgment are missing from many logistics and inventory decisions. Wisdom and sound judgment often fall prey to the tyranny of self-imposed deadlines and/or prevailing fads and philosophies. Ironically, "logic" has gone missing from a lot of logistics.

God and Inventory?

The root word for logic is "**logos**", a Greek word meaning, "Word of God, divine reasoning, wisdom, balance". I lean heavily on Heavenly resources and Wisdom for working through complex supply chain tradeoffs. I have prayed many times for insights into our clients' highly complex supply chain and inventory strategies. (Our Japanese team, a joint venture of LRI Japan and Mitsubishi, is called the LogOS™ Team in honor of this

⊛RightChain™

approach.) In my experience, the balance, Wisdom, and common sense that flow from God's Word is absent from most business settings; yet It always yields the most prosperous results for all involved; even with inventory strategy.

One of the most famous stories in the Bible is an inventory strategy (Genesis 41). You may remember it. Joseph was in prison. Pharaoh, the King of Egypt had a disturbing dream. In the dream there were seven fat cows and seven gaunt cows. The gaunt cows ate the fat cows. Pharaoh and all the psychics and fortune tellers in Egypt could not interpret the dream. Joseph was summoned from prison to give the king an interpretation. God gave Joseph the interpretation and he shared it with the king.

There would be seven years of prosperity followed by seven years of famine. A man of wisdom was to be promoted to manage both. Joseph turned out to be that man. He devised a strategy to put some of the excess grain from the prosperous years in inventory to be used during the years of famine. The inventory strategy saved two nations, Egypt and Israel, and got a young man promoted to prime minister of the most powerful nation on earth.

God may have even invented lean. When the Israelites were wandering in the desert God gave them one day's worth of food every day, except the day before the Sabbath when He gave them two days' worth (Exodus 16:4-5). No more. No less. The food was literally manna from Heaven and would spoil if any was held in inventory. It was a test to see if they would follow God's instructions. Yes, He has processes for inventory strategy. Our job is to ask Him what they are for each situation and follow them.

He gave other instructions regarding inventory. He discourages hoarding (Mathew 6:19). He encourages developing business strategy before supply chain and logistics strategy (Proverbs 24:27), and applying His Wisdom when building warehouses (Proverbs 24:3). He rewarded ten young people for holding enough inventory of the right type in the right place to take advantage of a once in a lifetime opportunity (Matthew 25:1-13). He gave us forewarning of the growing number, intensity, and destruction of the "natural" disasters we now frequently read about (Matthew 24); and recommended diversification. because we don't know what's coming next (Ecclesiastes 11:2).

I try to remember to ask the Lord to reveal His Best inventory strategy for our clients. So far, we are $1 Billion to the good. Sometimes the answer is more. Sometimes the answer is less. Sometimes the answer is the same but in different places. Sometimes the answer is the same but different types. ***There has never been a silver bullet, panacea, or miracle inventory diet.*** It has always been a process, not an event. The strategy has always been different depending on the current and future business, logistics, economic, and cultural conditions.

☙RightChain™

Supply Chain

If that's "logistics", what's a "supply chain"? There seems to be just as much confusion about the definition of "supply chain" as there is about "logistics". Everyone seems to have their own. Here's ours. *A supply chain is the infrastructure of factories, warehouses, ports, highways, railways, terminals, modes of transportation and information systems connecting consumers and suppliers.*

Supply Chain Logistics

Putting the two together, supply chain logistics is the flow of material, information and money in the infrastructure of factories, warehouses, ports, information systems, highways, railways, terminals, and modes of transportation connecting consumers and suppliers. Logistics is what happens in the supply chain. Logistics activities (customer response, inventory management, supply, transportation, and warehousing) connect and activate the objects in the supply chain. I like to use a sports analogy. *The supply chain is the stadium and logistics is the game.*

Supply Chain Logistics Activities

In 1990 I developed Frazelle's Framework of supply chain logistics to help professionals understand and implement supply chain strategies. The framework is guiding the supply chains of many of the world's largest supply chain organizations and is the foundation for the supply chain curriculums of many academic programs.

Our framework is an answer to a desperate prayer for a means to explain to a mean-spirited, cynical CEO of a very large chemical company why he did not need the $15 million warehouse and hundreds of jobs he had just promised on TV to a downtrodden local economy. I needed a way to explain that a large warehouse was not the best answer to the absence of a customer service policy, excess inventory, disintegrated sources of supply, and uncoordinated transportation operations. In contrast, the answer was to eliminate or minimize the need for physical warehousing by (1) developing a **customer service** policy, (2) determining the amount of **inventory** required to support that service policy, (3) optimizing and coordinating their **supply** and manufacturing schedules, and (4) optimizing the **transportation** operations. Whatever role remained for physical inventory (5) defined the requirements for **warehousing**. Once that supply chain strategy was developed, the excess inventory and need for additional warehousing were eliminated, customer service was improved, and profits increased.

Thus emerged our five-pointed star model (Figure 4.1) of supply chain logistics – the sequential activities of customer service, inventory management, supply, transportation, and warehousing. Each individually and in conjunction with one another ultimately determine inventory requirements. We will

≈RightChain™

consider them one by one and then in conjunction with one another.

Our RightChain™ framework goes one level deeper in explaining the activities of supply chain logistics. That next level is presented in Figures 4.2 and 4.3.

According to our RightChain™ model, customer service optimization (RightServe™) is accomplished through customer valuation, segmentation and optimization (RightSales™); SKU valuation, segmentation, and optimization (RightSKUs™); pricing optimization (RightPrice™); customer satisfaction optimization (RightSat™); and customer service policy optimization (RightTerms™).

Inventory optimization (RightStock™) is accomplished through forecast optimization (RightCast™); lot size optimization (RightLots™); fill rate optimization (RightFill™); inventory planning optimization (RightPlan™); and inventory deployment optimization (RightPloy™).

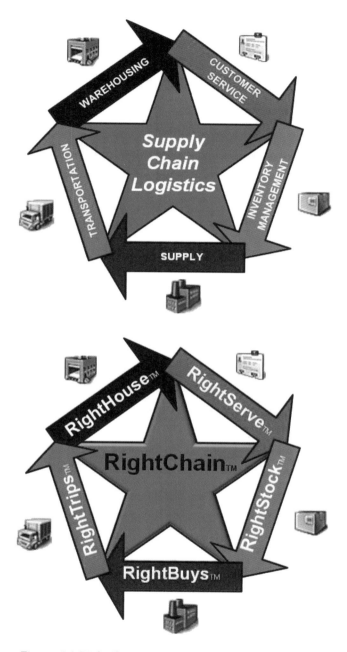

Figure 4.1 RightChain™ Model of Supply Chain Logistics

🌀RightChain™

Supply optimization (RightBuys™) is accomplished through supplier valuation (RightCard™); supplier optimization (RightCore™); supplier service policy optimization (RightTerms™); allocation optimization (RightSource™); and supplier integration (RightLinks™).

Transportation optimization (RightTrips™) is accomplished through network optimization (RightMaps™), shipment optimization (RightShip™), fleet optimization (RightFleet™), carrier optimization (RightLines™), and freight optimization (RightFreight™).

Warehouse optimization (RightHouse™) is accomplished through receiving optimization (RightIns™); putaway optimization (RightPuts™); storage optimization (RightStore™); order picking optimization (RightPick™); and packing optimization (RightPack™).

Each of these sub-activities also have a major impact on inventory requirements, which we will consider as well.

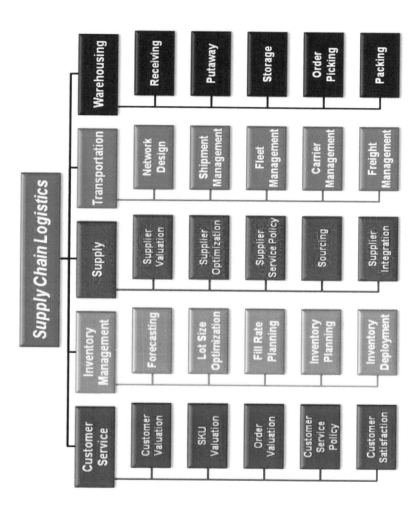

Figure 4.2 Frazelle's Framework of Supply Chain Logistics - Descriptive

⊛RightChain™

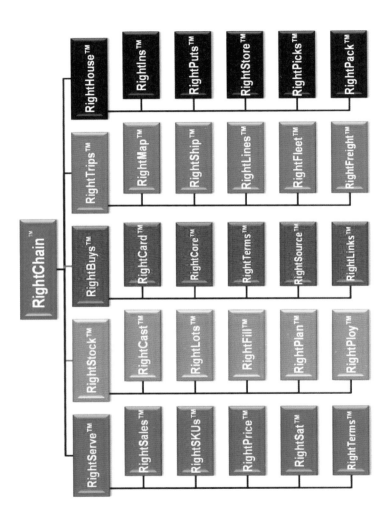

Figure 4.3 RightChain™ Framework of Supply Chain Logistics

4.2 Inventory and Customer Service

Our RightChain™ Model begins with customer service for two reasons. First, a humble attitude of service is a basis for supply chain success. High levels of customer service are a common denominator in superior supply chain leadership. Quite simply, **leaders serve**. Christ Himself, the Leader of leaders, encouraged us along these lines when He told us that He had not come to be served, but to serve. Second, the constraints developed as a part of a customer service policy are the underpinnings for supply chain and inventory optimization.

It is fascinating to observe the faces and body language of managers and directors in RightChain™ kickoff meetings. The bodily and facial slumping, sets in almost immediately. Most assume the project will be all about "cutting heads" and heavy expense reductions through declining service offerings. That's not what RightChain™ or RightStock™ are about. **They and we are about determining the most profitable way and level of inventory to service customers and to take the burden of supply chain logistics off sales and marketing, so they can focus on sales and marketing**. In the end, our strongest proponents are often sales and marketing teams, dealer support groups in automotive service parts, chefs in our restaurant projects, doctors in our healthcare programs, etc. **The RightChain™ begins with service!**

Customer service and customer service policies link supply chain logistics externally to the customer base and

RightChain™

internally to sales and marketing. Customer service is optimized when the customer service policy (CSP) that maximizes the financial and service performance of the organization is identified, implemented, and maintained.

Optimizing customer service (RightServe™) includes customer valuation, segmentation and optimization (RightSales™); SKU valuation, segmentation, and optimization (RightSKUs™); pricing optimization (RightPrice™); customer satisfaction optimization (RightSat™); and customer service policy optimization (RightTerms™), all of which play a major role in determining inventory requirements.

An example customer service policy developed as part of a supply chain and inventory strategy project for a major semi-conductor manufacturer is presented in Figure 4.4. The figure illustrates many of the dimensions of a customer service policy that impact inventory requirements including fill rate, response time, returns, value added services, minimum order quantities, and consolidation. Of those, fill rate and response time nearly always have the greatest impact on inventory requirements.

Service Segment	Customer-Item Class	Fill Rate	Response Time (Hours)	Returns Policy	Value Added Services	Minimum Order Quantity	Consolidation
I	A-A	99.0%	24	100%	Custom	None	Custom
II	A-B	95%	24	100%	Custom	None	Custom
III	A-C	85%	48	100%	Custom	None	Custom
IV	B-A	97%	24	50%	Limited	1000+	Partial
V	B-B	90%	48	50%	Limited	500+	Partial
VI	B-C	80%	72	0%	None	100+	Partial
VII	C-A	90%	48	50%	None	5000+	Partial
VIII	C-B	75%	72	0%	None	1000+	Partial
IX	C-C	50%	96	0%	None	500+	Partial

Figure 4.4 Example Customer Service Policy for a Semi-Conductor Company

⊛RightChain™

Inventory and Fill Rate

As explained earlier, fill rate requirements go a long way toward determining overall inventory requirements. Simply put, all things being equal, the higher the fill rate requirement, the higher the inventory level required to support it. The higher inventory levels are the result of additional safety stock inventory.

An example inventory and fill rate analysis from a recent engagement in the health and beauty industry is provided in Figure 4.5. Note that as fill rate increases (from 50% to 99.95%) the required inventory investment increases accordingly from $4,646,094 to $8,644,548. At the same time, lost sales cost declines from a high of $17,953,234 at a 50% fill rate to a low of $17,953 at a 99.95% fill rate.

The current inventory investment in the example was $8,300,000 and the lost sales cost was $3,949,712. The inventory investment that should have yielded a 99.9% fill rate only yielded an 87% fill rate. The discrepancy turned out to be a major mis-deployment of inventory.

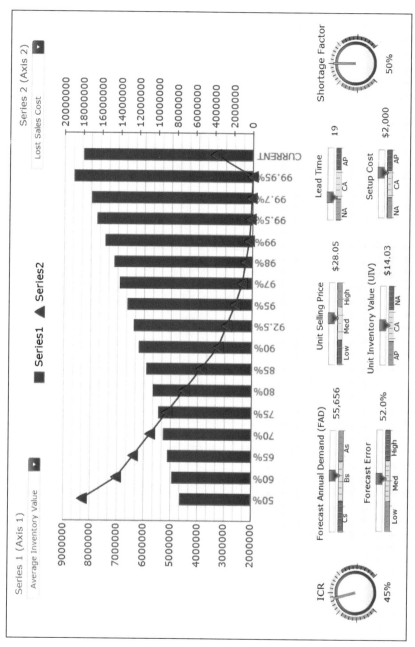

Figure 4.5 Inventory vs. Fill Rate for a Health & Beauty Company

Inventory and Response Time

Customer response time requirements are also a significant contributor to inventory requirements. If required customer response times are longer than supplier and/or manufacturing lead times; no inventory is required. If that is not the case, then the shorter the response time requirement, the greater the inventory requirement. The increase is normally due to additional facilities required in close proximity to customers, and their associated inventory deployment requirements. As described earlier, the greater the number of inventory stocking locations, the greater the inventory requirements.

Inventory and Delivery Frequency

Delivery frequency is an important but often overlooked dimension of customer service policy. In general, more frequent deliveries yield better customer service and lower inventory levels. Delivery frequencies also determine lot sizes. Daily shipping equates to a daily lot size. Weekly shipping equates to a seven day lot size. The greater the lot size, the greater the inventory. More frequent deliveries generate higher transportation costs; the result of more frequent trip setups and greater travel distances.

Delivery frequency optimization (DFO) determines the delivery frequency – days between deliveries – that minimizes total logistics cost including transportation and inventory carrying cost. An example delivery frequency optimization devised for a large retail client is presented in Figure 4.6. Note that the greater the delivery frequency, the less inventory and retail space required to support the delivery policy. For this particular store location the optimal delivery frequency is 3 days between deliveries. The optimal solution is based on the store's daily sales, inventory density, distance from the warehouse, delivery cost per mile, and setup cost per delivery.

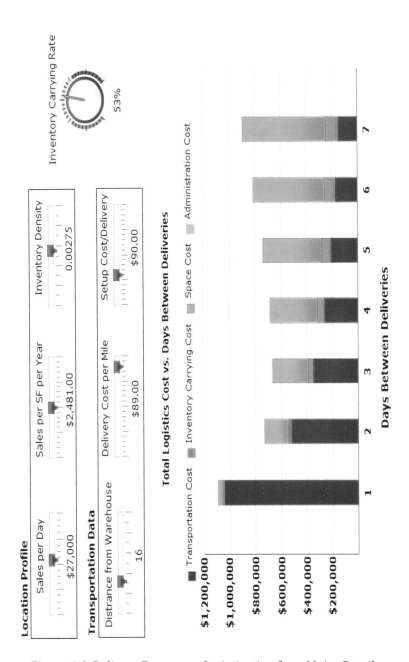

Figure 4.6 Delivery Frequency Optimization for a Major Retailer

4.3 Inventory and Inventory

The second consideration in RightChain™ supply chain strategy development is inventory planning and management. Many assume the goal is to minimize the amount of inventory in the supply chain. That's not the goal. ***The goal is to determine the amount and mix of inventory that satisfies the requirements of the customer service policy and maximizes the financial performance of the supply chain.*** (We covered inventory optimization in Chapter 3.)

4.4 Inventory and Supply

The third set of RightChain™ decisions work in the area of supply. Supply is the process of producing or acquiring inventory sufficient to meet the targets established in inventory planning. The objective of supply management is to maximize the financial performance of production and/or acquisition while meeting the availability, response time, and quality requirements stipulated in the customer service policy and the inventory strategy. Since we have to make up gaps between supplier service and customer service with excess inventory and/or excess transportation costs, we need high performance suppliers who have the same (or greater) passion for customer service that we do.

Optimizing supply (RightBuys™) includes supplier valuation (RightCard™), supplier optimization (RightCore™), supplier service policy (RightTerms™), sourcing (RightSource™),

☜RightChain™

and supplier integration (RightLinks™). Those activities and their related decisions have a major impact on inventory requirements. Inefficient and unreliable suppliers with unpredictable leadtimes require us to carry excess inventory to cover their unreliability. Efficient and reliable suppliers supplying fast moving items with predictable demand allow us to take advantage of inventory reduction strategies such as cross docking and non-stop putaway.

Of all the supply-based decisions, sourcing, the allocation of business to suppliers and the related choice of purchasing terms, has the greatest impact on inventory. Unfortunately, of all the groups working in supply chain management, the sourcing and procurement organization is the least likely to be trained in inventory and supply chain management. To help make the connection in one client engagement, I recommended that sourcing and procurement move from their posh offices at headquarters to a set of cubicles in the warehouse overlooking the receiving dock. It was highly unpopular but highly effective. The people making the decisions could literally see (and sometimes hear and feel) the impact of their decisions.

We also help make the sourcing and inventory connection with sourcing optimizations that take into consideration the full set of parameters and buying terms that impact the financial, service, operations, and inventory performance of the buy. An example RightBuys™ sourcing optimization is presented in Figure 4.7.

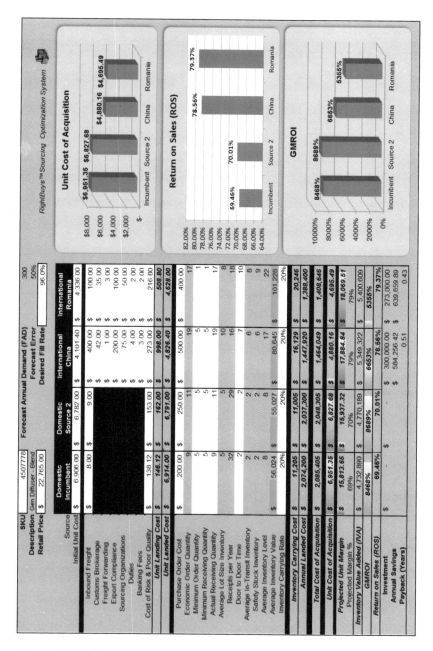

Figure 4.7 RightBuys™ Sourcing Optimization for a Global Manufacturer

RightChain™

The example is from a recent supply chain strategy project in which the client was considering moving a large portion of their supply base to China and eastern Europe. In fact, the far-sourcing train had a lot of momentum when we were asked to help them consider the full supply chain ramifications of the decision.

As we typically do, we put each of their SKUs through our RightBuys™ Sourcing Optimization System. The optimization revealed that about 1/3 of the SKUs needed to remain domestically sourced, about 1/3 should be sourced in China, and the remaining 1/3 in eastern Europe.

Initial Unit Cost (First Cost)

Our analysis considers the three main cost elements of sourcing decisions. The first is the **initial unit cost** (sometimes referred to as the first cost) offered from each supplier. Those costs ranged from $4,101 per unit from the eastern European candidate to $6,906 per unit from the incumbent domestic suppler.

Landing Costs

The second group of costs are **landing costs.** Landing costs include inbound freight, customs brokerage, freight forwarding, export compliance, sourcing organization fees, duties, banking fees, and the cost of poor quality. In this case the unit landing costs ranged from $146 with the incumbent domestic supplier to $998 per unit from the Chinese supplier. The sum of unit landing cost and initial unit cost is the **unit landed cost**. Unit landed cost ranged from $4,628 to $6,914.

Inventory Carrying Costs

The third set of costs is inventory carrying costs. Some sourcing analyses consider landing cost implications, but few incorporate inventory carrying cost. We include the three buckets of inventory described earlier – safety stock, lot size, and pipeline inventory. As expected, inventory carrying costs from the international suppliers are much higher. The inventory carrying costs for each option range from $11,005 from a candidate domestic supplier to $20,246 from the Romanian supplier.

Total Cost of Acquisition

The sum of inventory carrying and landing cost is the **total cost of acquisition**. The total cost of acquisition ranges from $1,408,646 to $2,085,405. The unit cost of acquisition ranges from $4,695 from the Romanian supplier to $6,951 from the domestic incumbent.

It is rare for one sourcing option to dominate the evaluation criteria, but that was the case here. The eastern European option provided the lowest total acquisition cost, the highest project margin, the highest return on sales, the highest inventory value added, and the shortest payback.

RightChain™

4.5 Inventory and Transportation

The fourth set of RightChain™ decisions are in the area of transportation. The goal of transportation is to link sources of supply with customers, within the guidelines of the customer service policy, and achieving the best possible financial performance. In that way, transportation is an integral part of a supply chain strategy. Transportation is not merely a non-value added, inconsequential, expense line item whose manager's sole focus is to reduce expenses to the bare bones via hard core carrier negotiations.

Transportation and the CFO

A few years ago we worked with a large frozen food company. A group of us were in the executive board room waiting for the CEO to show up for our meeting. I was seated next to the CFO. While we were waiting he decided to take me through their financial statements. He was especially proud of their expense statement for the prior twelve months. He insisted on showing me that all but one of their expense items had been reduced as compared to the prior year. He indignantly pointed out that the single line item that had increased in comparison to the prior year was transportation. (I think he thought I was single-handedly responsible for that increase because I was a supply chain consultant.)

He then asked me what I thought they should do about their transportation expenses. Instead of replying right away I asked him what had happened to profit during the period that transportation expenses had increased. He said that profit was up. I asked him what had happened to market share during the period in which transportation expenses had increased. He said that market share was up. I asked him what had happened to customer satisfaction during the period when transportation expenses had increased. He said that customer satisfaction had increased. He got upset and impatiently asked, "But Dr. Frazelle, what should we do about transportation expenses? They are increasing." I said, "It looks to me like you should spend even more on transportation, because it seems to be working." That was the last time he spoke to me. Six months later it was the last time he spoke to anyone in the company because he was let go. I expect it was because he was overly determined to reduce every single expense in the company, even at the cost of lower profits, lower revenue, and poor capital utilization.

Before he was let go, this same CFO tried to push his expense reduction point with my partner, Juan Rubio. The CFO was insisting we help them reduce transportation expenses by 20%. To get our point across and to point out how ridiculous the CFO had become, Juan suggested to him, "Just transport the orders 80% of the way to the customer. Drop the product off one exit before the customer's exit. Call them and let them know they can pick up the product there."

It's not just about the expenses. Transportation is a key component in an overall supply chain strategy. The supply chain strategy exists to maximize the financial and service performance of the company.

Transportation optimization (RightTrips™) includes network optimization (RightMaps™), shipment optimization (RightShip™), fleet optimization (RightFleet™), carrier optimization (RightLines™), and freight optimization (RightFreight™).

Those transportation activities and their related decisions have a significant impact on inventory requirements. We consider two of them in detail below.

Inventory and Network Design

Supply chain inventory levels logically increase as the number of stocking locations in the network increase. The increase is a result of the greater number of deployment decisions, the associated errors, and the resulting additional safety stock.

An example supply chain network optimization for a biotechnology client is depicted in Figure 4.8. Note that as the number of facilities increases, inventory carrying cost increases. However, total transportation cost decreases. The sum of those two, the total logistics cost is minimized with four facilities.

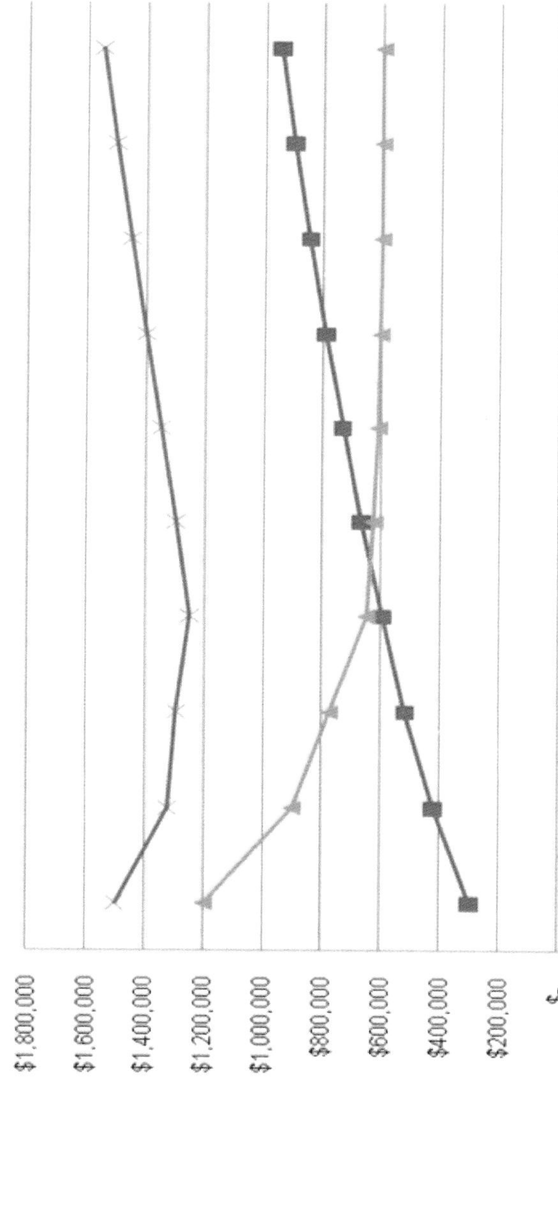

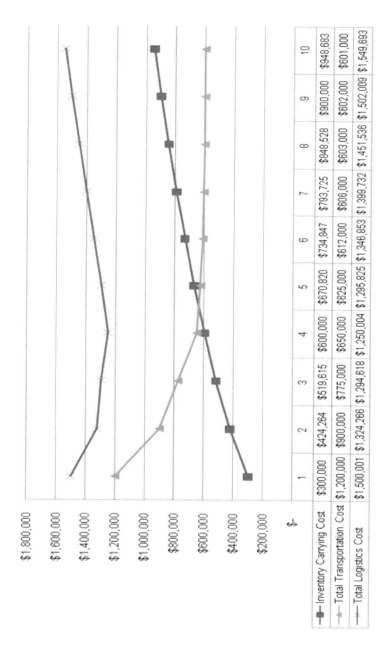

	1	2	3	4	5	6	7	8	9	10
Inventory Carrying Cost	$300,000	$424,264	$519,615	$600,000	$670,820	$734,847	$793,725	$848,528	$900,000	$948,683
Total Transportation Cost	$1,200,000	$900,000	$775,000	$650,000	$625,000	$612,000	$606,000	$603,000	$602,000	$601,000
Total Logistics Cost	$1,500,001	$1,324,266	$1,294,618	$1,250,004	$1,295,825	$1,346,853	$1,399,732	$1,451,536	$1,502,009	$1,549,693

Figure 4.8 Inventory Investment and Supply Chain Network Design

Inventory and Shipping Frequency

Inventory levels logically decrease as shipping frequency increases. Shipping frequency determines lot size. Daily shipping requires a daily lot size. However, daily shipping requires a daily trip and preparation for the trip. Weekly shipping requires a weekly lot size. However, weekly shipping requires one trip a week instead of seven. An example shipping frequency optimization for retail delivery is presented in Figure 4.9. For the particular store in the example, daily shipping is optimal and results in $665,417 in transportation cost, $27,375 in transportation setup cost, $165 in inventory carrying cost and $692,957 in total logistics cost. For this particular commodity, transportation costs dominate inventory carrying costs and therefore dictate shipping frequency.

A summary analysis for all stores is presented in Figure 4.10. Note that the optimal shipping frequency is greater for those stores with higher sales rates and in closer proximity to the distribution center.

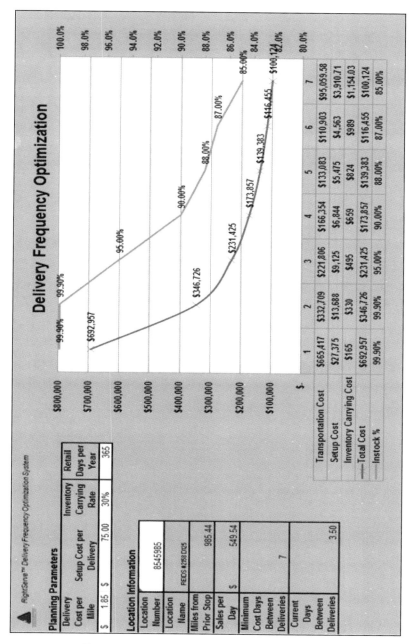

Figure 4.9 Inventory and Shipping Frequency

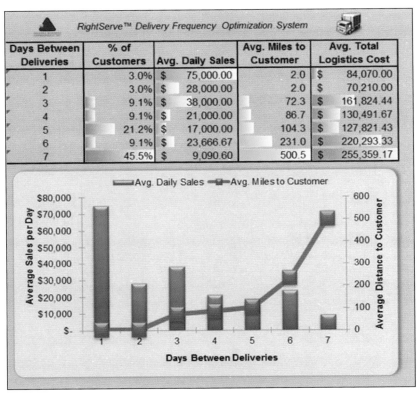

Days Between Deliveries	% of Customers	Avg. Daily Sales	Avg. Miles to Customer	Avg. Total Logistics Cost
1	3.0%	$ 75,000.00	2.0	$ 84,070.00
2	3.0%	$ 28,000.00	2.0	$ 70,210.00
3	9.1%	$ 38,000.00	72.3	$ 161,824.44
4	9.1%	$ 21,000.00	86.7	$ 130,491.67
5	21.2%	$ 17,000.00	104.3	$ 127,821.43
6	9.1%	$ 23,666.67	231.0	$ 220,293.33
7	45.5%	$ 9,090.60	500.5	$ 255,359.17

Figure 4.10 Shipping Frequency Optimization Summary

Inventory and Modes of Transportation

Choosing transportation modes also plays a significant role in determining inventory requirements. The slower the transportation mode, the longer the lead time, the greater the pipeline inventory and associated safety stock inventory, and the higher the inventory carrying costs. However, the slower the mode, the lower the transportation costs. Shipments with high value relative to their weight and cube are best shipped with faster transportation modes, and shipments with low value relative to their weight and cube are best shipped with slower, less expensive modes.

Mode optimization, RightModes™, identifies the transport mode that meets the response time requirements and yield the best financial performance A mode optimization conducted for a major health and beauty company is presented in Figure 4.11. As expected, the inventory carrying cost for the two air carriers is significantly lower while the freight costs are significantly higher. The optimal mode choice depends upon the preferred financial performance metric. In this case, Ocean Carrier 5 minimizes the Total Logistics Cost and the Supply Chain Value Added. Air Carrier 1 maximizes Gross Margin Return on Inventory and Inventory Value Added.

🞲RightChain™

LRI's RightModes™
Mode Optimization System™

Product Parameters	Unit Inventory Value	Unit Selling Price	Inventory Carrying Rate	Forecast Annual Demand	Fill Rate	Leadtime Forecast Error	Weight (pounds)
	$ 4,000.00	$ 7,000.00	35%	2,400	95.00%	45.00%	12

Mode/Carrier Parameters	Air Carrier 1	Air Carrier 2	Ocean Carrier 1	Ocean Carrier 2	Ocean Carrier 3	Ocean Carrier 4	Ocean Carrier 5
Transit Times Door-To-Door	7	12	28	35	30	21	21
Frequency of Shipment Arrival	7	5	7	28	14	21	21
Freight Cost Door-to-Door ($/pound)	$ 25.00	$ 20.00	$ 14.00	$ 11.00	$ 10.50	$ 11.50	$ 11.50
Transportation Setup Cost ($/shipment)	$ 1,200.00	$ 1,500.00	$ 3,000.00	$ 3,600.00	$ 2,400.00	$ 3,800.00	$ 1,900.00
On-Time Arrival Percentage	95.00%	93.00%	94.00%	90.00%	92.00%	94.50%	87.50%
Tardiness (days)	0.50	0.30	4.00	6.30	7.30	8.30	9.30
Inventory Carrying Cost	$ 156,508	$ 235,879	$ 530,663	$ 754,969	$ 601,494	$ 473,036	$ 479,535
Lost Sales Cost	$ 360,000	$ 360,000	$ 360,000	$ 360,000	$ 360,000	$ 360,000	$ 360,000
Total Freight Cost	$ 720,000	$ 576,000	$ 403,200	$ 316,800	$ 302,400	$ 331,200	$ 331,200
Transportation Setup Cost	$ 62,571	$ 109,500	$ 156,429	$ 46,929	$ 62,571	$ 66,048	$ 33,024
Total Logistics Cost	$ 1,299,079	$ 1,281,379	$ 1,450,292	$ 1,478,698	$ 1,326,466	$ 1,230,283	$ 1,203,759
TLC per Unit	$ 541.28	$ 533.91	$ 604.29	$ 616.12	$ 552.69	$ 512.62	$ 501.57
GMROI	1610%	1068%	475%	334%	419%	533%	526%
LGMROI™	1320%	878%	379%	265%	342%	442%	438%
Inventory Value Added™	$ 7,043,492	$ 6,964,121	$ 6,669,337	$ 6,445,031	$ 6,698,506	$ 6,726,964	$ 6,720,465
Supply Chain Value Added™	$ 5,540,921	$ 5,558,621	$ 5,389,708	$ 5,361,302	$ 5,513,534	$ 5,609,717	$ 5,636,241

Figure 4.11 Inventory and Modes of Transportation

4.6 Inventory and Warehousing

The fifth and last set of RightChain™ supply chain strategy decisions has to do with warehousing. It's my personal favorite, but I have to admit it's the last logistics activity that should be considered when developing a supply chain strategy. First, *a clever trip through the first four RightChain™ initiatives may eliminate, should minimize, and will correctly determine the need for warehousing as opposed to letting the warehouse play its habitual role as the physical manifestation of the lack of supply chain coordination, integration, and planning*. Second, the warehouse is like a goalie in a soccer game. Like it or not, it's the last line of defense, and needs to be designed accordingly. Third, we need customer service, inventory management, supply, and transportation requirements from the supply chain to properly plan and operate the warehouse. Finally, we may learn that a third-party should operate the warehouse.

Optimizing warehousing includes optimizing receiving (RightIns™), putaway (RightPuts™), storage (RightStore™), order picking (RightPick™), and packing (RightPack™). Those five individually and in conjunction play a major role in determining supply chain inventory requirements.

Inventory and Receiving

One of the principal ways receiving and putaway impact inventory requirements is via dock-to-stock time, the elapsed

🦑 RightChain™

time from when a receipt arrives on premises until it is ready for picking and shipping. A few years ago we were asked to assist a large apparel retailer with their supply chain strategy. We toured their main distribution center during one of the initial visits. I noticed their receiving dock looked especially full. I asked them what their dock-to-stock time was. They shared proudly that it was 96 hours. I shared from our benchmarking that 24 hours was a norm; 8 hours was a top quartile result, and 2 hours was world-class. They were defensive and said they had looked into systems to reduce dock-to-stock time, but they could never produce an acceptable return on investment. I asked them how much inventory was sitting on the dock. It was $8 million worth of inventory. I asked them what range of investment proposals they received for the material handling systems required to help them reduce cycle time to 24 hours. Quotes were in the range of $2 million. I did some quick math and calculated that by reducing their dock-to-stock time by 75% they could reduce their inventory by $6,000,000. I asked them, "Wouldn't it make sense to spend $2 million to take $6 million out of inventory or to reduce inventory carrying costs by $2 million per year at a 33% inventory carrying rate?" They shared that they had tried to compute an ROI based on labor savings alone and had not considered inventory savings. That re-consideration launched one of the nation's most successful supply chain strategies.

Inventory and Storage

Two features of storage have a major impact on inventory levels: inventory accuracy and storage space utilization.

First, high levels of inventory accuracy are achieved through high putaway and picking accuracy, ABC cycle counting, disciplined housekeeping, and real time transactions. Without high degrees of trust in the numbers used to support it, inventory and supply chain planning break down quickly.

Second, optimal storage utilization helps enforce healthy inventory management. In our early work with Honda their warehouse space utilization was in excess of 98%. When it came time to implement a new warehouse management system, the warehouses were so full that there was no room to move product to create the space needed to re-label and reconfigure racking to accommodate the new system. I suggested they delay implementation and reset the storage utilization capacities to 85% - what it should be for most warehouses. They asked me what they would do with their excess inventory. I half-jokingly suggested they rent a warehouse in a remote location where space was especially cheap. Any product occupying space over and above 85% should be shipped to that remote location. When the 85% occupancy had been established, they could install the WMS.

I was a bit surprised to learn later that they had accepted my recommendation. The remote warehouse occupied more

RightChain™

than 500,000 square feet. The Japanese president received the monthly bill and dispatched an associate to look at the remote operation. It turned out the material was essentially excess safety stock generated by their forecasting system. The excess had previously been stuffed into their facing distribution centers. Pulling the material out of the forward DCs helped them see and experience just how much excess safety stock their inventory plan was producing. The visualization and the bill from the third-party helped to motivate a highly successful makeover of their forecasting process and system.

Summary

Space and time do not permit the opportunity to share all the facets of supply chain logistics and their impact on inventory. We have shared many of the most important ones. A summary of the factors and their impact on inventory follows in Figure 4.12.

Factor	More inventory is required if...
Fill Rate	fill rate requirements are **higher**
Response Time	response time requirement are **faster**
Shipping Frequency	shipping is **less frequent**
Return Rates	return rates are **higher**
SKUs	there are **more SKUs**
Forecast Accuracy	forecasting is **less accurate**
Leadtime	leadtimes are **longer**
Lot Size	lot sizes are **larger**
Deployment	**more stocking locations** are utilized.

Visibility	visibility is **poorer**.
Transportation Mode	modes are **slower**.
Loss and Damage	loss and damage are **higher**.
Inventory Accuracy	inventory accuracy is **poorer**.

Figure 4.12 Tying it all together.

These supply chain principles are like logistics laws of gravity; they just are. To think otherwise is to live in supply chain denial.

Several years ago one of our clients retained us to help them with a space dilemma. The distribution group was running overtime, working at 106% occupancy in their main DCs, and renting five off-site, overflow DCs. Their CFO was peeved by the overages. Their distribution group complained that they were only allocated enough space to accommodate the inventory levels projected by their merchandising group. Their sales and turn forecast projected that there was sufficient space.

We were "invited" to help resolve the conflict. We found the merchandising group had jury-rigged their inventory turn forecasts. Regardless of true trends in sales or turns, their projection always suggested that the current space was adequate. They took the true sales forecast and forecasted the turns required to avoid renting outside space. They never met those turn rates.

RightChain™

To help resolve the issue I took the inventory requirements factors we just discussed - fill rate, the number of SKUs, forecast accuracy, etc. - and taught a short seminar for both groups on the impact each factor would have on inventory. Once they all agreed on the factors in principle I took them through their particular trends. Fill rate requirements were higher. Forecast accuracy was lower. Leadtimes were longer. There were many more SKUs. Supply chain visibility was poorer. After a few minutes the head of merchandising made me stop, He admitted that they got the point. The business unit president insisted that I go on. It was very awkward, but she insisted that I finish the presentation revealing that every single one of their supply chain trends suggested they would continue to need even more inventory and space than they already had. Basically, the head of merchandising had been caught red handed manipulating the turn forecast.

4.7 Inventory and the Supply Chain

A recent client requested we develop the Wrong Chain Model (Figure 4.13) to help them understand the self-inflicted sub-optimization, internal conflict, and excess inventory in their supply chain. It also happens to be the reason why there is self-inflicted sub-optimization, internal conflict, and excess inventory in nearly every supply chain.

Think about a typical supply chain including sales, manufacturing, sourcing, transportation, and warehousing.

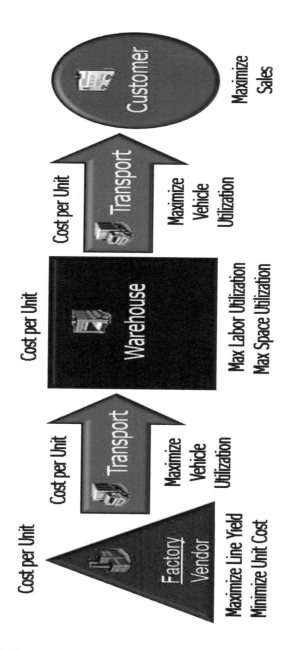

Figure 4.13 Wrong Chain Model of Supply Chain Sub-Optimization

First stop... sales. Let's assume the sales force creates the forecast and works on commission. What's the worst thing that could happen to a commission sales person? Running out of product. So, guess what kind of forecast they will most likely turn in? You guessed it... an inflated forecast that will not run out of product. The result... more safety stock inventory than you know what to do with.

Second stop... manufacturing. How are most plant managers measured? The large majority of plant managers are evaluated based on the unit cost, plant yield, and/or machine utilization within the four walls of the plant. How do you go about achieving those objectives? Long production runs creating lots of inventory are the norm.

Third stop... sourcing. How are most buyers measured? The large majority of buyers are measured based on how low a price they can pay a vendor for the product. How do you get a low price? Large purchase quantities creating lots of inventory are the norm.

Next stop... transportation. How are most transportation managers measured? Most transportation managers are evaluated based on transportation cost as a percent of sales, cost per mile, and/or vehicle utilization. How do you minimize transportation cost and maximize vehicle utilization? By making sure the outbound containers and vehicles are as full as possible, in other words by maximizing the in-transit inventory.

Last stop... warehousing. How are most warehouse managers measured? Most warehouse managers are measured on space utilization and labor cost per unit. How do you maximize space utilization? By filling up the warehouse. How do you minimize the labor cost per unit? By holding orders and releasing large batches of work to the warehouse floor. Those two objectives work together to increase four-wall inventory.

Is it any wonder there is excess inventory in nearly every supply chain?

One day I received a call from the Chief Operating Officer of a large food company. He said they were struggling with the inventory levels in their supply chain strategy. I asked him if he minded if I guessed at what their problem was. I took him through the illogic of what I just exposed. There was an awkward silence on the line and then he burst out laughing. I asked him why he was laughing. He said it was because they had been struggling with their excess inventory levels for more than a year, had paid millions in unfruitful software licenses and consulting fees, and in less than a minute I had diagnosed their inventory ills without ever stepping foot in one of their offices or operations. He said he thought I was a supply chain genius.

I'm not a genius. What I shared with him and just shared with you is the root cause of the large majority of inventory ills in every supply chain. The illness is the misalignment of metrics between elements of the supply chain.

RightChain™

There are many and various mistakes in the wrong chain model. Sometimes it's helpful to learn from mistakes.

One mistake is silos of decision making. We correct that mistake in the RightChain™ Supply Chain Integration Model (Figure 4.14) by housing all supply chain activities under one decision making roof. Another major mistake in the wrong chain model is the focus on unit cost reduction achieved primarily by maximizing the utilization of individual resources in the supply chain. RightChain™ corrects that by developing and implementing an overarching objective function to minimize total supply chain cost while simultaneously meeting the requirements of the customer service policy.

Our RightChain™ Supply Chain Integration Model uses optimization to portray the mission of an integrated supply chain and to determine the proper role and schedule for each supply chain activity. The primary role of the contributing activities is to meet the integrated and optimized supply chain schedule. For example, plant managers, who formerly focused almost exclusively on reducing manufacturing unit cost and increasing machine utilization now focus on schedule attainment: the schedule that is best for the entire chain. Buyers, who formerly focused almost exclusively on "cost avoidance" typically accomplished through large buy commitments from far-away places now focus on the most profitable buy and inbound product delivery schedule that is best for the entire supply chain. Transportation managers who formerly focused almost exclusively on squeezing every penny out of carrier negotiations and/or making sure that every container, vehicle, and driver is fully utilized now focus on making sure the pickup and delivery schedule that is best for the entire supply chain is reliably executed. Warehouse managers who formerly focused almost exclusively on making sure every slot, vehicle, dock, and operator were fully utilized now focus on executing the shipping and receiving schedule that is best for the entire supply chain and operating storage capacity that best accommodates the inventory requirements for the entire supply chain. Sales is now held accountable to the accuracy of their forecasts. *The resulting inventory is the right level of inventory.*

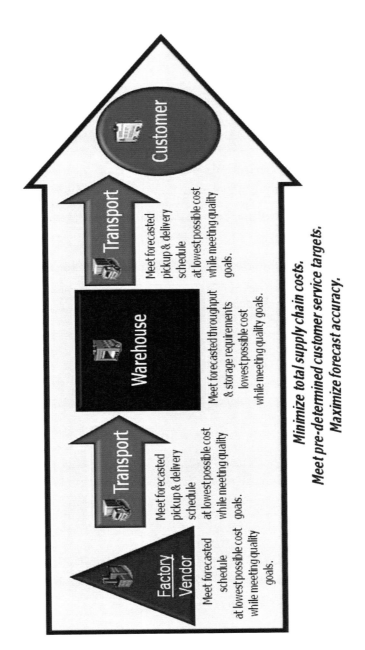

Figure 4.14 RightChain™ Supply Chain Integration Model

4.8 Beyond S&OP

Sales and operations planning (S&OP) receives a lot of attention as a potential panacea for inventory optimization and rationalization. Done properly it can help along those lines. The key, usually missing, is "done properly".

Over the last few years I have attended, reviewed, and even facilitated several S&OP meetings. Sometimes sales is not there. Sometimes operations is not there. Sometimes planning is not there. Sometimes inventory is not discussed. Sometimes logistics is not involved. Sometimes the meeting morphs into a seminar, or worse. Sometimes the meeting doesn't happen. Reliable data is the exception rather than the rule. The decision support tools necessary to answer tough questions are rarely available. Though seemingly a "standard" in the industry, I have found S&OP to have as many different meanings as there are companies.

Despite those disappointments, I was encouraged recently at two client sites. Pratt & Whitney Canada coined the term "SIOP" for Sales, Inventory, and Operations Planning. Coca-Cola Consolidated coined the term "T&OP", Transportation & Operations Planning. They both recognized something is missing from "S&OP" and launched out on their own.

As I mentioned early on, there are a variety of valid perspectives on inventory – (1) financial, service, and operations; (2) strategic, tactical, and execution; (3) customer service, manufacturing, sourcing, transportation, and warehousing, Each of those perspectives needs to be addressed, optimized, and rationalized in the "S&OP" process and meetings. In addition, though traditional S&OP has focused primarily on inventory, the scope should be expanded to consider the total supply chain and its ability to support the financial and service requirements of the business. We developed the RightChain™ planning process to help companies move beyond S&OP to integrated supply chain planning and optimization. The process is illustrated in Figure 4.15 and described in steps 1 through 7.

Cadence >	Daily	Weekly	Monthly	Quarterly	Annually
Time Frame >	EXECUTION	EXECUTION/TACTICAL	TACTICAL	TACTICAL/STRATEGIC	STRATEGIC
Participation >	Manager	Manager/Director	Director	Director/VP	Director/VP/C-Level
GATE >	I	II	III	IV	V
Demand & Requirements Rationalization					
Customer Response	Sales Orders Update → Shipping Update, MRP/DRP Update	→ Pre-Concensus Forecasting	→ Concensus Forecasting, Demand Planning	→ Customer Valuation, Customer Satisfaction, CSP Update, SKU Valuation	→ Long Range Demand Planning, Portfolio & Channel Strategy, Customer Service Policy, Customer Conference
Inventory	Inventory, ABC Cycle Count, Perpetual Inventory	Management RightChain™, Inventory Scheduling, Supply Signal Update	Director RightChain™, Smoothing, Concensus Planning, Inventory Planning	Executive RightChain™, Deployment Review, Material Flow Plan, Supply Chain Scoreboard Review	Strategic RightChain™, Network Strategy, Flow Strategy, Supply Chain Strategy
Capacity Optimization & Supply					
Manufacturing, Supply, Transportation, Warehousing	Production, Purchase Orders, Bills & Manifests, Receipts & Pick Sheets	Manufacturing Scheduling, Supply Scheduling, Transportation Scheduling, Warehouse Scheduling	Manufacturing Planning, Supply Planning, Transportation Planning, Warehouse Planning	Manufacturing Review, Sourcing Review, Transportation Review, Warehousing Review	Long Range Capacity Strategy, Sourcing Strategy & Supplier Conference, Transportation Strategy & Carrier Conference, Warehousing Strategy & 3PL Conference
METRICS — Finance, Service, Inventory, Stability	Sales, OTD, POP, Inventory Accuracy, No. of Changes	Sales, OTD, POP, $s, Days, Turns, No. of Changes	EBIT, ROS, Cash, ROIC, OTD, POP, IVA, GMROI, IPC, $s, Days, Turns, % Changes	EBIT, ROS, Cash, ROIC, OTD, POP, IVA, GMROI, IPC, $s, Days, Turns, % Changes	EBIT, ROS, Cash, ROIC, OTD, POP, IVA, GMROI, IPC, $s, Days, Turns, % Changes

Figure 4.15 RightChain™ Planning Process

RightChain™

1. **Cadence and Gates.** Supply chain requirements and capacity must be rationalized and optimized in the short, middle, and long term. Therefore, the RightChain™ program works in daily (Gate I), weekly (Gate II), monthly (Gate III), quarterly (Gate IV), and annual (Gate V) timeframes accordingly.

2. **Organization Levels.** All levels of the organization are impacted by, should participate in, and be held accountable to RightChain™ decisions. Participation by levels including manager, director, and executive are highlighted in the diagram. Meeting types are labeled as Management RightChains™, Director RightChains™, and Executive RightChains™ to reflect the nature of the decisions considered in the work sessions.

3. **Players.** At each gate in the RightChain™ planning process, appropriate representatives from the major multi-disciplinary areas of the corporation should meet. For example, Executive RightChain™ meetings would include the CFO/VP Finance, COO/VP Operations, CEO/President, CSMO/VP Sales and Marketing, CMO/VP Manufacturing, and CSCO/VP Supply Chain. Director RightChain™ meetings would include their counterparts at the director level. Management RightChain™ meetings would include their counterparts at the management level.

4. **Demand and Requirements.** Forecasted demand has typically focused on customer demand in units or dollars and is often developed solely by sales. Customer demand should

be vetted through consensus forecasting, and should be extrapolated to include all supply chain units of measure including pieces, cases, pallets, cube, weight, and loads. The elements of the customer service policy such as fill rate, response time, delivery frequency, etc. also act as requirements on the supply chain and should be considered as well. All of these are reflected in the swim lane labeled "Demand and Requirements".

5. **Supply and Capacity**. Capacity in "S&OP" has typically focused on unit manufacturing capacity. Capacity should reflect not only manufacturing capacity, but also sourcing capacity, transportation capacity, warehousing capacity, I/T capacity, and financial capacity to fund inventory investments. Each of those is a potential bottleneck in total supply chain capability. Each potential bottleneck is considered in the Supply and Capacity swim lane.

6. **Performance Measures**. Traditional S&OP performance metrics are focused on operational inventory indicators like inventory days-on-hand or turns. However, a supply chain schedule, plan, and strategy impacts many more metrics including inventory financial performance, EBIT, ROIC, workforce productivity, supply chain asset utilization, revenue, total supply chain cost, customer service, complexity, etc. Our RightChain™ Scoreboard considers the full range of inter-related metrics and is illustrated in Figure 4.16. It is organized by metrics related to providing

ۑRightChain™

customers with excellent customer service, employees with a great place to work, and shareholders with excellent financial returns.

7. **Tools and Data.** One of the typical hindrances to successful S&OP meetings is the lack of real-time decision support tools to answer the tough and sometimes meeting-squelching questions that arise. We developed the RightChain™ Analytics Portal to support real-time data mining and decision making at each planning stage. A RightChain™ Analytics Portal home page from a recent client engagement is provided in Figure 4.17.

Year 2010 · Month July · Channel Grocery · Category Waters · State TN

Category	Sub-Cat		Selling	Planning	Manufacturing	Sourcing	Transportation	Warehousing	Delivery	Merchandising	SUPPLY CHAIN
Customers / Service	Quality		94.0% PSQ	56.0% Fcast Accuracy	99.0% PMQP	81.0% PSQP	92.0% PDP	72.0% PWHQP	98.0% PDP	93.0% PMCQ	72.0% POP
	Cycle Time		1.9 SCT	4.7 PCT	7 MCT	14.3 POCT	8.2 TCT	2.4 YTS, WDCT	5.4 DCT	12.8 MCT	17.3 SCCT
	On Time		93% % on-time	92% % adherence	92% % adherence	92% % OT POs	92% % loads on-time	92% % order on-time	92% % loads on-time	92% % merch on-time	92% SCOT
Employees / GPTW	Safety		4,250.0 MH/I	7,653.0 MH/I	3,822.0 MH/I	8,788.0 MH/I	9,145.0 MH/I	9,987.0 MH/I	9,650.0 MH/I	8,998.0 MH/I	9,001.0 MH/I
	Satisfaction		81.0% % yes	91.0% % yes	93.0% % yes	94.0% % yes	91.0% % yes	81.0% % yes	79.0% % yes	98.0% % yes	65.0% % yes
	Development		9.2 out of 10	8.1 out of 10	9.3 out of 10	8.5 out of 10	8.7 out of 10	7.3 out of 10	9.2 out of 10	8.8 out of 10	8.7 out of 10
Shareholders / Finance	Cost	$	1.23 $s/case	1.22 $s/case	2.99 $s/case	0.99 $s/case	1.88 $s/case	2.11 $s/case	1.82 $s/case	4.21 $s/case	12.24 $s/case
	Capital	$	12,000,000 $s	48,000,000 $s	207,000,000 $s	2,000,000 $s	50,000,000 $s	60,000,000 $s	70,000,000 $s	80,000,000 $s	529,000,000 $s
	ROIC		6.00% SROA	12.00% GMROII	33.00% GMROA	21.00% GMROII	9.00% GMROA	45.00% GMROA	33.00% DROA	8.00% MROA	19.00% SCROIC
Productivity	Labor		67 orders/MH	43 $s/FTE	78 cpmh	34 cpmh	124 cpmh	112 cpmh	100 cpmh	21 cpmh	12 cases/FTE
	Space		0.998 GM/cube	0.876 GM/cube	0.776 GM/SF	0.601 GM/cube	0.398 GM/cube	21.3 cases/SF	0.511 GM/cube	0.991 GM/cube	18.99 cases/SF
Utilization	Labor		90.0% % labor util	91.0% % labor util	91.0% % labor util	65.0% % labor util	73.0% % labor util	82.0% % labor util	82.0% % labor util	93.0% % labor util	81.0% % labor util
	Capital		28.0% % buy util	34.0% % buy util	81.0% % prod util	99.0% % buy util	34.0% % fleet util	44.0% % cap util	39.0% % fleet util	89.0% % buy util	82.0% % cap util
	Space		91.0% % space util	80.0% % space util	78.0% % space util	79.0% % space util	77.0% % space util	80.0% % space util	89.0% % space util	89.0% % space util	80.0% % space util
TOTAL		$	18.91 TSLC/PSO	13.45 TTC/PTO	11.10 TMC/PMO	9.97 TSC/PSO	8.88 TTC/PTO	9.12 TWC/PWHO	11.10 TDC/PDO	12.55 TMCC/PMO	28.93 TSCC/PtcOrder
	Practices		2.1 out of 5	2.8 out of 5	2.8 out of 5	2.8 out of 5	2.8 out of 5	2.8 out of 5	2.8 out of 5	2.2 out of 5	2.4 out of 5
	Complexity		2,000 orders	500 SKUs	3,000 SKU-lines	2,000 SKU-suppliers	3,000 SKU-stops	5,000 locations	1,000 SKU-stops	10,000 accounts	26,500 complexity
	Risk		4.1 out of 5	2.8 out of 5	3.1 out of 5	3.1 out of 5	4.8 out of 5	3.5 out of 5	3.2 out of 5	2.5 out of 5	3.1 out of 5

Figure 4.16 RightChain™ Supply Chain Scoreboard

🐌 RightChain™

RightChain™		RightServe™ Service Optimization	RightStock™ Inventory Optimization	RightBuys™ Supply Optimization	RightTrips™ Transportation Optimization	RightHouse™ Warehouse Optimization	RightChain™ Supply Chain Optimization
DATA	Data Warehousing	Sales Order File	Inventory File		Transportation File	Warehouse File	Supply Chain Data Warehouse
	SKUs	Customer360	Profit360, Excess360	Supplier360, PO360	Lane360, Carrier360, Mode360	Location360	SupplyChain360
	Paretos	Customers, Orders	SKUs, Programs, Modules, Planners	Suppliers, Purchase Orders	Lanes, Modes, Carriers	Locations, Operators	Regions
PROFILING							
PERFORMANCE	Scoreboards	Customer Service Scoreboard	Inventory Scoreboard	Supply Scoreboard	Transportation Scoreboard	Warehouse Scoreboard	Supply Chain Scoreboard
	Metrics	GM%, POP, On-Time	GMROI, Excess, Fill	GM%, PPOP, On-Time	Cost/Lb-Mile, On-Time%	TWC, Inv Acc, Ship Acc	TSCC, TSCC/PO
PRACTICES	Practice Gaps	RightServe™ Customer Service Practices Assessment	RightStock™ Inventory Practices Assessment	RightBuys™ Supply Practices Assessment	RightTrips™ Transportation Practices Assessment	RightHouse™ Warehouse Practices Assessment	RightChain™ Supply Chain Practices Assessment
	X-Rays	RightServe™ X-Ray	RightStock™ X-Ray	RightBuys™ X-Ray	RightTrips™ X-Ray	RightHouse™ X-Ray	RightChain™ X-Ray
ACTIONS	Optimization	GM% Review	Inventory Optimization	Sourcing Optimization	Mode Review	Slotting Analysis	Current vs Future State Total Supply Chain Cost
	Infrastructure	Customer Svc Policy	Develop Fcast Acc Data	Leadtime Reviews	TMS ROI	3PL Review	
	Compliance	CRMS Assessment	IMS Reqts	Import Review	Export Control	OSHA Review	ISO 9000 Review
	Organization	Svc Training Simulation	Inventory Planner Skills	Buyer Training	Hire Dir. Of Compliance	DC Reorganization	S&OP Trial

Figure 4.17 RightChain™ Analytics Portal Home Page

Glossary

Allocated Inventory (ALI)
Untouchable inventory set aside for and dedicated to specific customers, channels, purposes, and/or business units.

Annual Demand (AD)
The number of units requested for an item during a year. It looks backward over the prior year and is strictly a historic

Assemble to Order (ATO)
An inventory, logistics, and supply chain concept made famous by Dell Computer in which assembly is delayed or postponed until the time an order is received.

Available Inventory (AVI)
On-hand inventory less allocated or committed inventory.
- AVI = OHI – ALI or AVI = OHI - CMI

Average Inventory Level (AIL)
The average number of units in inventory including safety stock inventory, lot size inventory, and lead time inventory.
- AIL = SSI + (LS/2) + [(L x (FAD/365)]

Average Inventory Value (AIV)
The average investment in inventory including safety stock inventory, lot size inventory, and lead time inventory.
- AIV = AIL x UIV

Average Leadtime Demand (ALD)
The average demand during a leadtime.
- ALD = L x (FAD/365)

Average Replenishment Quantity (ARQ)
The average replenishment quantity (ARQ) is the average size of lot size replenishments derived by dividing the total replenishment quantity over a particular period of time by the number of replenishments received during that time.

Bill of Material (BOM)
Hierarchical assembly structure.

Buckets of Inventory (BOI)
A reference to the purposeful allocation, tracking and planning for inventory in three distinct buckets - safety stock inventory (SSI), lot size inventory (LSI), and pipeline inventory (PI).

Changeover Cost (COC)
Cost to setup (prepare or changeover) a machine or production line to make a production run for a particular item or change between items.

Committed Inventory (CMI)
Untouchable inventory held specifically or allocated specifically for customers, business units, and/or channels of business

Consignment Inventory (CSI)
Inventory that is physically on our premises but not fiscally on our books; it is still owned by and sometimes managed by the vendor. Hence, this inventory is sometimes referred to as vendor managed inventory (VMI).

Contingency & Disaster Inventory (CDI)
Exists to cover unexpected situations outside the realm of those covered by traditional safety stock inventory. Those situations would include scenarios like natural disasters, labor strikes, and other exceptional supply chain disruptions.

Days-on-Hand (DOH)
The ratio of the average inventory value (AIV) to current of forecasted daily usage.
- $DOH = AIV/(FAD/365)$

Economic Order Quantity (EOQ)

(1) Manufacturing EOQ is the run quantity or batch size that minimizes the sum total of inventory carrying cost and setup cost. (2) Procurement EOQ is the purchase quantity that minimizes the sum total of inventory carrying cost and procurement cost.

- $EOQ = \{[\ 2 \times FAD \times SUC\ ] / [\ UIV \times ICR\ ]\}^{1/2}$

Fill Rate (FR)

The % of customer demand satisfiable from on-hand inventory

Forecast Annual Demand (FAD)

(1) Forecasted annual demand for an item (2) predicted demand in units for the upcoming 12 month period (3) the forecasted (or expected) annual number of units requested by customers

Forecast Leadtime Demand (FLD)

Forecasted demand during a leadtime.

- $FLD = L \times (FAD/365)$

Gross Margin Return on Inventory (GMROI)

The financial return on inventory investments expressed as the ratio of the annualized gross margin to the average inventory investment.

- $GMROI = GM/AIV = [\ (USP - UIV) \times FAD\ ] / AIV$

Hedge Inventory (HDI)

(1) Inventory purchased as a hedge against potential price increases. (2) Hedge inventory (HDI) exists to cover potential sharp price increases and/or shortages in critical commodities.

Inventory Carrying Cost (ICC)

Annualized cost of carrying inventory.

- $ICC = AIV \times ICR$

Inventory Carrying Rate (ICR)
Percentage per year applied to average inventory value to annualize cost of carrying inventory usually including opportunity cost of capital, storage, handling, insurance, taxes, obsolescence, loss, and damage.

Inventory Quality Ratio (IQR)
The percentage of the total inventory investment that is in active SKUs is termed the inventory quality ratio (IQR), a very helpful indicator of inventory performance, acting akin to a bad debt ratio for banks.
- $IQR = (AIV\ Active)/AIV$

Inventory Policy Cost (IPC)
The sum of inventory carrying cost and lost sales cost.
- $IPC = ICC + LSC$

Inventory Turn Ratio (ITR)
The number of times inventory turns each year, typically expressed as the ratio of annual sales at cost to average inventory value.
- $ITR = (FAD \times UIV)/AIV$

Inventory Value Added™ (IVA)
Inventory value added is an EVA-like metric applied to inventory.
- $IVA = GM - ICC$

Leadtime (L)
Manufacturing leadtime is the elapsed time from when a manufacturing order is released to the factory until product is available for sales from manufacturing. Procurement leadtime is the elapsed time from when an order is released to a vendor until the product is available for sales.

Leadtime Demand (LD)
Demand during a leadtime.
- $LD = L \times (FAD/365)$

Leadtime Forecast Error Percentage (LFEP)
The absolute value of the forecast error percentage over a leadtime.

Life Cycle Inventory (LCI)
Life Cycle Inventory (LCI) models allocate inventory to categories based on product maturities. Typical maturities include (1) Conception, (2) Infancy, (3) Adolescence, (4) Mature, (5) Decline, (6) Discontinue., (7) Burial.

Logistics
The flow of material, information and money between consumers and suppliers.

Lost Sales (LS)
Lost sales occur when the unsatisfied demand is lost. Lost sales are common in retail situations where there are many alternative outlets for a product.

Lost Sales Cost (LSC)
The potential sales lost due to out of stocks.
- LSC = [FAD x USP] x (1-UFR) x SF

Lot Size (LS)
The lot size(LS) (also known as the replenishment quantity (RQ) or the cycle stock (CS)) is the number of units that arrive in a replenishment lot or are produced in a manufacturing lot.

Maximum Inventory Level (MIL)
The sum of the economic order quantity, safety stock, and leadtime inventory.
- MIL = SSI + EOQ

Net Inventory (NI)
On-hand inventory less units on backorder (UOB).
- NI = OHI - UOB

Non-Value Added Inventory (NVAI)
Non-working, excess inventory. Inventory that is not adding value either as safety stock inventory, lot size inventory, or pipeline inventory.

- NVAI = TIL – VAI

On-Hand Inventory (OHI)
(1) the most common inventory reference (2) the number of units of inventory physically on-hand in storage

Order-up-to-Level (OUL)
The level of inventory a replenishment quantity should yield when it is placed.

Out of Stock (OOS)
Stockout situation covered via lost sales, substitution, or back order.

Purchase Order Cost (POC)
Cost of planning, placing, tracking, and paying a purchase order. Used in economic order quantity computation.

Raw Material Inventory (RMI)
Inventory that has not been converted, changed, processed, or in any way changed in value.

Reorder PointROP
The inventory position at which an order is placed. Normally is equal to the safety stock plus the average leadtime demand.

- ROP = SSI + LD

Replenishment Cycle Time (RCT)
Elapsed time between replenishments. The annual number of replenishments is the 365 days divided by the average elapsed time between replenishments.

Return on Invested Capital (ROIC)
Return on invested capital (ROIC) is the ratio of operating profit to invested capital. It encompasses all elements of revenue, expense and capital.

Review Time Period (RTP)
The time between inventory reviews.

Safety Stock Inventory (SSI)
Literally the amount of stock on-hand when a replenishment arrives. Safety stock is a function of forecast error, desired fill rate, and inbound delivery reliability. The model sets safety stock to the product of the normal inventory value associated with the desired fill rate and the standard deviation of leadtime demand.

Seasonality and Build Inventory (SBI)
Exists to level production and machine, line and plant utilization.

Setup Cost (SUC)
The cost to setup (prepare or changeover) a machine or production line to make a production run for a particular item or change between items. It is sometimes referred to as the changeover cost (COC). Used in economic order quantity computation.

Shortage Factor (SF)
Percent of unit selling price lost when out of stock. The default value is set as the margin %. Used in lost sales cost computation.

Standard Deviation of Leadtime Demand (SDLD)
A measure of the variability of leadtime demand.

Stock Keeping Unit (SKU)
A number or set of alpha numeric characters that reference a unique part or item, sometimes called a part number.

Supply Chain (SC)

The supply chain is the infrastructure of factories, warehouses, ports, information systems, highways, railways, terminals, and modes of transportation connecting consumers and suppliers.

Supply Chain Logistics (SCL)

The flow of material, information and money in the infrastructure of factories, warehouses, ports, information systems, highways, railways, terminals, and modes of transportation connecting consumers and suppliers.

Unit Fill Rate (UFR)

The % of total units requested by customers satisfiable from on-hand inventory

Unit Gross Margin (UGM)

The difference between the unit selling price and the unit inventory value. The higher the unit gross margin, the higher the cost of lost sales associated with that particular item.
- UGM = USP - UIV

Unit Inventory Value (UIV)

Unit cost of manufacturing (sometimes referred to as standard cost) or unit cost of purchase (sometimes referred to as unit cost of goods sold).

Units on Backorder (UOB)

The number of units outstanding on backorders.

Unit Selling Price (USP)

The unit selling price (USP) for an item is the price per unit paid by a customer for an item.

Value Added Inventory (VAI)

(1) inventory that is adding value such as safety stock that mitigates demand variability risk, lot size inventory that offsets setup and ordering costs, and pipeline inventory that corresponds to leadtimes (2) all inventory that is not excess or waste (3) the difference between total inventory and value-added inventory.

- VAI = TI - NVAI

Vendor Managed Inventory (VMI)

Inventory managed by and procured for us by vendors.

About the Author

Edward H. Frazelle, Ph.D.
President & CEO, Logistics Resources International
Executive Director, RightChain™ Institute

Dr. Frazelle is President and CEO of Logistics Resources International and founding director of The Logistics Institute at Georgia Tech. Logistics Resources International is a supply chain consulting firm with offices in Atlanta, Georgia; Tokyo, Japan; and San Jose, Costa Rica. As an educator, Dr. Frazelle has trained more than 50,000 professionals in the principles of world-class supply chains; as a consultant he has assisted more than 100 corporations and government agencies in North America, South America, Europe, Asia and Africa in their pursuit of world-class supply chains; as an author he has authored, co-authored, and/or contributed to seven books including *Supply Chain Strategy, World-Class Warehousing, Facilities Planning,* and *The Language of Logistics*; and as a professor he has lectured at Cornell, Northwestern, Waseda University, and the National University of Singapore. His books have been translated into six languages including Japanese, Chinese, Korean, Russian, Spanish, and Portuguese.

Dr. Frazelle is also the inventor of RightChain™, a supply chain strategy model guiding the supply chains in many of the world's largest corporations including Honda, Disney, BP, Hallmark, Nutrisystem, and United Technologies to name a few.

⊛RightChain™

RightChain™ projects have accounted for more than $2 BILLION in EBIT increase for LRI clients.

Dr. Frazelle's achievements have been recognized by the Council of Supply Chain Management's Doctoral Research Grant, the Warehousing Education and Research Council's Burr Hupp Fellowship, the Material Handling Institute's MHEF Fellowship, the Institute of Industrial Engineer's Armstrong Award, Kodak's Educational Grant, and General Motors Scholar Award. He was recently named Georgia Tech's Outstanding Professional Educator. He is a former president of the International Material Management Society and member of the board of directors for the Warehousing Education & Research Council. Dr. Frazelle holds his Ph.D. from Georgia Tech and masters and bachelors of science degrees from North Carolina State University.

Other Books by the Author

- *Supply Chain Strategy*
- *World-Class Warehousing and Material Handling*
- *Material Handling Systems and Terminology*
- *Facilities Planning*

Blogs and Sites by the Author

- RightChain.com
- InventoryStrategy.com
- WorldClassWarehousing.blogspot.com
- WorldClassTransportation.blogspot.com

About Logistics Resources International

Logistics Resources International is a supply chain consulting, professional education, and analytics firm. The firm was founded by Dr. Ed Frazelle to help organizations develop and implement supply chain strategies that maximize the financial, service, and operational performance of the enterprise.

Based on LRI's proprietary RightChain™ model of supply chain strategy, LRI offers supply chain consulting, supply chain seminars, decision support programs, and publications in supply chain strategy, customer service, inventory management, sourcing, transportation, and warehousing. To date, our clients have put more than $2 billion dollars on their bottom line through LRI projects. Our consulting programs have helped a number of clients receive their industry's most prestigious awards for supply chain excellence. Our principals are the leading subject matter experts in their fields, serving clients simultaneously as consultants, facilitators, and teachers.

We serve our clients from offices in Atlanta (LRI Global Headquarters and LRI North America); Tokyo, Japan (LRI Asia Pacific); and San Jose, Costa Rica (LRI Latin America); and from affiliates in Sydney, Australia (Logiworx) and Lima, Peru (GS1 Peru).

About RightChain™

✦RightChain™

Based on more than two decades of supply chain strategy consulting, executive education, and research, the RightChain™ program includes the definitions, methodology, tools, curriculum, principles, metrics, processes, and delivery mechanism required to address the major decisions in supply chain strategy development. The RightChain™ is successfully guiding the supply chains of large, medium, and small companies in nearly every major industry around the world and is responsible for more than $2 billion in bottom line impact through optimized combinations of sales increases, expense reductions, and capital utilization improvement. The RightChain™ typically puts between 1% and 5% of sales on the bottom line. It has been taught to more than 10,000 supply chain professionals in seven languages around the world.